OLSAT-E
TWO PRACTICE TESTS

2017 EDITION

GRADES 4 & 5 (5TH & 6TH GRADE ADMISSION)

GET READY FOR THE OLSAT-E:

**Two practice exams (each exam has 72 multiple choice questions)
**Detailed solutions to help your child avoid making the same mistakes
**Test-taking techniques to build confidence
**In-depth review of exam content

OLSAT®
PRACTICE TEST

Grade 5 (6th Grade Entry) & Grade 4 (5th Grade Entry)
LEVEL E

Tests 1 & 2

Copyright © 2017 by Origins Publications

Written and Edited by:
Gifted and Talented OLSAT Test Prep Team

ISBN:978-0997768053

Origins Publications
New York, NY, USA

Email:info@originspublications

ABOUT ORIGINS PUBLICATIONS

Origins Publications and the OLSAT® Test Prep Team helps students develop their higher-order thinking skills while also improving their chances of admission into gifted and accelerated learner programs.

Our goal is to unleash and nurture the genius in every student. We do this by offering educational and test prep materials that are fun, challenging and provide a sense of accomplishment.

Please contact us with any questions.

info@originspublications.com

Contents

PREPARATION GUIDE

Part 1. Introduction to the OLSAT-E

The Otis Lennon School Ability Test (OLSAT) is an important exam; the more you know about it, the better you will fare. This guide offers an overview of the types of questions that are likely to be on the test, some test-taking strategies to improve performance during preparation and on test day, and sample OLSAT© tests that students can use to test their knowledge and practice their test-taking skills.

Why the OLSAT-E?

Many gifted and talented programs and highly-selective public schools across the USA require students to pass an exam in order to be admitted to the school or program. The OLSAT-E is often used as an assessment tool or admissions test in 4th and 5th grade for entry into 5th and 6th grade of highly-competitive programs and schools.

Who Takes The OLSAT-E?

Fourth and fifth graders who want to gain admission to fifth and sixth grade in a gifted and talented program, or highly-selective school. The OLSAT-E can also be used as an assessment tool by teachers to decipher which students would benefit from an accelerated or remedial curriculum.

When Does the OLSAT Take Place?

This depends on the school district you reside in, or want to attend. Check with the relevant school/district to learn more about test dates and the application/registration process.

OLSAT© Level E Overview

The OLSAT® is a test of abstract thinking and an individual's ability to reason logically. It measures verbal, quantitative, and spatial reasoning ability. In taking the OLSAT®, students will be evaluated on their ability to perceive information accurately, understand relationships and patterns among objects, reason through abstract problems, apply generalizations, and recall and evaluate information.

The OLSAT® covers topics that students may not see in school, so kids will need to think a little differently in order to do well. A student's stress management and time management skills are also tested during the nearly hour-long exam.

Length

The OLSAT® Level E test is a 40-minute test.

Format

The entire test is made up of 72 multiple choice questions. The questions are distributed as follows:

VERBAL		NONVERBAL	
Verbal Comprehension		**Figural Reasoning**	
Antonyms	4	Figural Analogies	6
Sentence Arrangement	4	Figural Series	6
Sentence Completion	4	Pattern Matrices	6
Verbal Reasoning		**Quantitative Reasoning**	
Arithmetic Reasoning	4	Number Inferences	6
Logical Selection	4	Pattern Matrices	6
Inferences	4	Number Series	6
Verbal Analogies	4		
Verbal Classification	4		
Word/letter matrices	4	**TOTAL QUESTIONS**	72

Test Sections

The test consists of verbal material and nonverbal material. The verbal material consists of verbal comprehension and verbal reasoning questions, while the nonverbal material consists of figural reasoning and quantitative reasoning questions.

Verbal Material

VERBAL COMPREHENSION QUESTIONS

The verbal comprehension questions are aimed at measuring students' ability to gather and manipulate information from language. In particular, these questions seek to evaluate how students understand the way words and sentences relate to each other, and also how students interpret nuances in language.

There are three types of verbal comprehension questions:

✓ **Antonyms:** These questions require students to search for the opposite meaning of a given word within the answer choices provided. In particular, this group of questions aims to evaluate a student's vocabulary skills. Ultimately, these questions require a sophisticated understanding of vocabulary because students have to not only comprehend a word, but also understand it enough so that they can recognize its true opposite.

✓ **Sentence Arrangement**: These questions provide students with sentences that have been mixed up. Looking at this jumbled set of words, students must piece the words together to compose a complete thought. These questions assess a student's ability to understand the structure of language by asking them to take fragmented parts and, from them, create a whole.

✓ **Sentence Completion**: With these questions students will have to "fill in the blank(s)." The answer options outline a number of words that could be used to complete a given sentence. However, students must choose the words that create a complete, logical sentence.

VERBAL REASONING QUESTIONS

The verbal reasoning component of the test measures a student's ability to comprehend patterns, relationships, and context clues in writing in order to solve a problem. In order to be successful in answering these questions, students must be able to fully understand what a question is asking, as well as make inferences based on what they have read.

The verbal reasoning questions on the test are composed of six different question types:

✓ **Arithmetic Reasoning**: These verbal problems incorporate mathematical reasoning. Some questions assess basic concepts, including counting, and estimation. Others assess more sophisticated concepts such as reasoning and solving word problems. The main skill tested here is the ability to create mathematical problems from language and to solve those problems.

✓ **Inferences**: Students will be provided an argument or scenario and, based on the information provided, must discern an appropriate conclusion. These questions rely on a student's ability to evaluate which parts of the provided information are absolutely necessary for reaching the correct conclusion.

✓ **Logical Selection**: In order to find the answers to these questions, students have to apply logical reasoning to uncover the best answer. These questions often asks students to consider which answer *might* be correct, versus which answer options are *always* correct. Being able to make that distinction is key.

✓ **Verbal Analogies:** These questions ask students to consider the relationship between a pair of words, then apply this relationship to another pair of words. Students' ability to correctly uncover these relationships is key to answering these type of questions.

✓ **Verbal Classification**: With these questions, students must look at a series of words or concepts and identify which one does not fit with the others. In answering this type of question, students must be able to evaluate the relationships among words.

✓ **Word/letter matrices:** These questions provide students with a matrix of letters or words. Students must perceive the pattern or relationship among these words in order to supply a missing letter or word.

Non-Verbal Material

FIGURAL REASONING QUESTIONS

The purpose of these questions is to measure a student's ability to reason their way through non-language based scenarios. These questions take a more visual format than the verbal questions, incorporating geometric figures instead of words. Students will be expected to find the relationship between numbers or objects in a pattern, to predict and create what the next level of the pattern will look like, and generalize the rules they discover.

There are four figural reasoning question types:

- ✓ **Figural Analogies**: Like verbal analogies, these questions require students to identify the relationship of a given pair. With these questions, however, students are asked to examine the relationship between figures instead of words. Once students have uncovered this relationship, they then must apply this rule to a second pair of figures. This question type assesses the student's ability to infer a relationship between a pair of geometric shapes and select the shape that is related to the stimulus in the same way.

- ✓ **Figural Classification**: In these questions, students must examine a group of figures and identify a pattern or principle that links those figures. Then, students must conclude which of the answer choices follows this same principle.

- ✓ **Figural Series**: With this series of questions, students must look at a series of geometric figures, discern a pattern within the series, and find the 'missing' drawing/shape in the pattern.

- ✓ **Pattern Matrices**: This question asks the student to supply a missing element in a matrix of geometric shapes. These questions test a student's ability to discern rules in a pattern and evaluate how those rules govern a series of geometric figures.

QUANTITATIVE REASONING QUESTIONS

These questions evaluates a student's ability to discern patterns and relationships in order to solve problems with numbers. This section requires that students be able to predict outcomes based on their knowledge of mathematics.

There are three types of quantitative reasoning questions:

- ✓ **Numeric Inferences**: Using computation skills, students will have to determine how two or three numbers are related. Once they have uncovered this relationship, students will have to apply this rule to another pair or trio of numbers.

- ✓ **Number Matrices**: For these questions, students must examine numbers in a matrix and determine what principle or rule links those numbers. Then, they must apply this rule to figure out what number should be placed in a given blank.

- ✓ **Number Series**: Students must examine a sequence of numbers and determine a pattern that governs those numbers. They will then apply that pattern in order to predict what comes next.

Part 2. Using This Book

You have made an important first step towards ensuring your child will do her best on test day by purchasing this book. This Preparation Guide offers general strategies your child can use to tackle the test. Your child can also prepare for the exam by taking the practice test in this book.

Origins Publications ©

Performance on the practice test can help identify a stu-dent's weaknesses and allow your child to focus on questions that most need to be reviewed.

When to Start Studying?

Every family and student will approach preparation for this test differently. There is no 'right' way to prepare; there is only the best way for a particular child and family. Some take the 'cram' approach, loading up on as many hours as possible before the test date. Other parents think too much focus on preparation may create anxiety in their child that could backfire on test day. In this case, a more low-key approach may work best.

With that said, repeated exposure to the format and nature of the test will help a student prepare for this challenging test. We suggest students, at minimum, take one practice test (preferably under timed conditions) and spend a minimum of 8-10 hours working through OLSAT® type questions.

As they say, knowledge is power! And preparing for the OLSAT also gives students a chance to know what they are up against. This alone can help a fifth-grader not panic on test day when faced with unfamiliar and perplexing questions. The OLSAT measures a student's academic performance but also his ability to manage time efficiently and capacity to keep his wits under pressure.

Part 3: Exam Preparation and Test-Taking Strategies

Preparing for the OLSAT in many ways follows the same process as preparing for any other exam—your child needs to review the concepts he or she already knows and boost skills in areas that he or she is unfamiliar with. You can diagnose your child's weaknesses by analyzing her scores on the practice test in this book. Then, focus study time on reviewing and practicing more of the question types that your child finds tricky or regularly stumbles on.

General Test Taking Strategies For OLSAT® Level E Test

The OLSAT® Level E does not just test your child's knowledge and skills in specific verbal and non-verbal areas, but also her test-taking skills. If your child knows the material on which she will be tested and is familiar with test-taking techniques and strategies, it will certainly improve her chances of doing well on the exam.

Help your child prepare for the test by using the following tips and strategies.

✓ KNOW THE TEST

The content and required pacing on this test is very challenging for a fifth grader. A student will need to sustain focus throughout the test. Because of this, it is important that your child is familiar with the format, nature and structure of the exam, and that he or she works on sample questions and takes practice tests in timed conditions.

As a general test preparation strategy, we recommend that you first review each question type with your child and ask him or her to solve practice questions without a time restriction. Then, spend time analysing the answers and explanations (both incorrect and correct) for each question.

In order to succeed on the test, a student must keep calm and learn to use time wisely. That's why we recommend that students take several timed practice tests, which helps build stamina and confidence, as well as ensures that a student does not waste time on test day panicking about the unknown! A practice test also helps a student get used to reading each question carefully but quickly, and figure out the best and fastest way to transfer answers and mark the bubbles in the answer sheet. For example, practicing the simple technique of shading the bubbles quickly and efficiently can help a student gain a minute or two during the test.

Use the scores on the practice tests to identify subject areas or question types where your child is struggling. If you have limited time to prepare, spend most energy reviewing areas where your child is encountering the majority of problems.

✓ DON'T LET DIFFICULT QUESTIONS UNDERMINE CONFIDENCE

Be prepared for difficult questions on the test from the get go! The OLSAT® is not given in an 'adaptive' format -- where each subsequent question increases in difficulty. The make-up of the exam is as follows; about half of the OLSAT® Level E is made up of "easy" questions, the answers to which most fifth graders will know. More than a third of the questions will be of medium difficulty, and students who receive close to a 'mean' score will also answer these correctly. In general, a student's strategy should be to avoid thoughtless mistakes and to solve these questions relatively quickly. About 18% of questions are difficult for most students. The students who answer some or all of these questions correctly are the ones that have the highest chance of being admitted to the assessing program or school.

So what to do when stumped with a tough question? First, a student needs to stay calm and focused. She can spend some extra time (but not too much!) on the challenging question (knowing that there are easier questions ahead which can be answered faster). If she is still unable to figure out the answer, she should make an educated guess and move on to the next question.

✓ USE PROCESS OF ELIMINATION

If a student is stumped by a question, she can use the process of elimination. Firstly, eliminate obviously wrong answers in order to narrow down the answer choices. If still in doubt after using this technique, she can make an educated guess. Process of elimination is a key technique that helps improve the probability of selecting the correct response even if a student is not sure about how to answer a question.

✓ NEVER LEAVE AN ANSWER BLANK

On the OLSAT® test, no points are deducted for wrong answers. Therefore, when all else fails, educated guessing should be used as a strategy. When a student finishes the test and has time to spare, he should review the answer sheet to ensure EVERY question has a marked answer.

✓ MARK UP THE TEST

Mark up the booklet as much as you need to as you take the test. If you find something that looks important, underline it, make notes in the margins, circle facts, cross out answers that are wrong, and draw diagrams.

✓ USE TIME WISELY

The OLSAT® Level E asks students to answer 72 questions in 40 minutes. This means a student has just over 30 seconds to answer each question. On test day, a student should always be aware of the time. Scanning ahead and seeing how many questions remain in the test will help him or her gauge how much time to allocate for each question.

✓ DEVELOP FIGURAL REASONING SKILLS

On the nonverbal material, the object is to use clues to find specific patterns and relationships, and then to apply that relationship or pattern to the answer options to identify the correct one among five choices. This includes finding similarities and differences between items or sets of geometric figures, predicting the next step in a progression of geometric shapes, or supplying a missing element in a matrix. In order to improve at this aspect of the test, we suggest students spend time doing activities such as puzzles, Sudoku, chess and/or Rubik's cube, all of which help develop a child's ability to identify and interpret patterns.

✓ IMPROVE VOCABULARY & READING COMPREHENSION

The verbal material on the test is the most difficult to prep for as it requires a child to have a large vocabulary and excellent reading comprehension. This is built up over time by reading widely and analysing what is read. If your child is preparing well enough in advance, he can spend time on building vocabulary using flashcards or, even better, learning and reviewing roots, prefixes and suffixes of words. A student can use the other general test-taking strategies to improve his score on the verbal section even if his vocabulary is not strong. However, strengthening vocabulary is a potential way to do better on the test.

✓ IGNORE ALL DISTRACTIONS

You may have tried to re-create the exact test-taking atmosphere during practice exams. But when your child goes for the real thing she will be in a room with many other kids, maybe even someone with a cold who is sneezing or coughing. Tell her to ignore it all and concentrate on her test.

✓ MANAGE TEST DAY JITTERS

Avoid squeezing in a last-minute review. Instead, encourage your child to visualize his success and plan a reward for after the test is over. Encourage your child to think positive when there's a frustrating question. Freezing up and thinking all kinds of negative ideas will only kill confidence during the exam. Instead, teach your child to use positive self-talk, including "I've studied this," "I can do this," and "I can figure this problem out." If your child finds himself getting anxious, tell him to help himself relax by taking long, deep breaths.

● KEEP THINGS IN PERSPECTIVE

Yes, the OLSAT-E is an important exam, but it needs to be put in context. Tell your child that even if he does poorly on the exam, it is not the end of the world. His family won't stop loving him. He won't be less of a person. Perspective is important to perfor-mance. Of course your child should be serious about succeeding on the test. But he should not lose sight of other important aspects of life.

Strategies for the Final Days before the Exam

The weeks or months of preparation will soon pay off. You have worked hard, and the test is just a week away. Here are some tips for making sure things go smoothly in the home stretch.

The Week before the Test:

- Be sure you know exactly where you are taking the test. Get detailed directions. Take a practice transit trip so you know exactly how long it will take to get there.
- Review everything you have learned.
- Get quality sleep each night.
- Practice visualization - see yourself performing well on the test.

The Day before the Test:

- Get to bed early.
- Get light exercise.
- Get everything you will need ready: pencils/pens, a watch, admission materials/documentation, and water or any mints or snacks you would like to have along.
- Make a list of everything you need to bring so you don't forget anything in the morning.

The Day of the Test:

- Eat a light, healthy breakfast, such as yogurt and granola or a low-fat, low-sugar cereal and fruit.
- Dress comfortably. Wear layers so that you can take off a sweatshirt or sweater if you are too warm in the test room.
- Avoid squeezing in a last-minute review. Instead, visualize your success and plan your reward for after the test is over.
- Think positive!

What to Bring to the Test

- ✓ A watch
- ✓ Water
- ✓ Two number 2 pencils with erasers and two black or blue ink pens
- ✓ Sweatshirt or sweater

In a manila envelope, also bring the following to complete the admissions process:

- ✓ Copies of your child's most recent report card
- ✓ Copies of the 4th grade NYS Exam in ELA/ Math or ERB
- ✓ Copy of your child's end of the year 4th grade report card
- ✓ Self-addressed stamped envelope

OLSAT© Level E Practice Test 1

1.

The opposite of **follow** is:

A. answer   B. lead   C. chase   D. question   E. talk

2.

The drawings in the box go together in a certain way. Which drawing goes where you see the question mark?

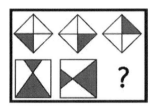

A   B   C   D   E

3.

The numbers in the box go together in a certain way. Which number goes where you see the question mark?

15	8	1
19	12	?

A. 10   B. 8   C. 7   D. 14   E. 5

4.

Which word does **not** go with the others?

A. chair   B. sofa   C. recliner   D. table   E. bench

5.

The drawings below form a series. Which drawing continues that series and goes where you see the question mark?

A   B   C   D   E

6.

Choose the words that **best** complete this sentence.

The bus had to _____ because the driver was _____.

- **A.** hurry — content
- **B.** stop — tired
- **C.** slow — eager
- **D.** speed — awake
- **E.** crash — uneasy

7.

What number is six more than three times eight?

  A. 45   **B.** 72   **C.** 24   **D.** 30   **E.** 10

8.

Light is to **dark** as **near** is to:

  A. beyond **B.** far **C.** close **D.** present **E.** distance

9.

If the words were arranged to make the **best** sentence, with which letter would the **first** word of the sentence begin?

day	have	all	you	where	been

  A. y   **B.** d   **C.** h   **D.** a   **E.** w

10.

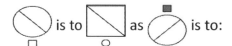 is to as is to:

  A   **B**   **C**   **D**   **E**

11.

A song cannot be sung without:

  A. an audience **B.** lyrics **C.** music **D.** instruments **E.** a band

12.

What number is missing in this series?   31   27   29   27   ?   27   25   27

    A. 30   **B.** 28   **C.** 27   **D.** 26   **E.** 29

13.

 is to as is to:

            A   B   C   D   E

14.

Which word does **not** go with the others?

    A. digest   **B.** consume   **C.** eat   **D.** ingest   **E.** devour

15.

The opposite of **truth** is:

    A. hope   **B.** fiction   **C.** healing   **D.** fact   **E.** history

16.

The drawings in the box go together in a certain way. Which drawing goes where you see the question mark?

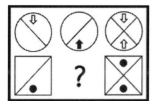

        A   B   C   D   E

17.

The numbers in the box go together in a certain way. Which number goes where you see the question mark?

2	6	18
3	9	27
4	?	36

    A. 10   **B.** 14   **C.** 11   **D.** 12   **E.** 8

18.

The words in the box go together in a certain way. Which word goes where you see the question mark?

flower	flea	flourish
?	animal	anemic

A. argue   **B.** absolute   **C.** angle   **D.** fanatic   **E.** float

19.

The numbers in each box go together following the same rule. Figure out that rule and then apply it to the third box. What number goes where you see the question mark?

12, 3   16, 4   20, ?   **A.** 7   **B.** 5   **C.** 10   **D.** 2   **E.** 12

20.

Carlos bought more tickets at the arcade than Olivia and Sofie combined. If Olivia bought fifteen tickets but gave three to Sofie, we know for certain that:

- **A.** Carlos bought twenty tickets
- **B.** Olivia is generous
- **C.** Sofie and Olivia end up with the same number of tickets
- **D.** Carlos bought more than fifteen tickets
- **E.** Sofie ends up with the most tickets

21.

The drawings below form a series. Which drawing continues that series and goes where you see the question mark?

       ?

                       A   **B**   **C**   **D**   **E**

22.

Tiger is to **stripe** as:

- **A.** dalmatian is to spot
- **B.** polar bear is to white
- **C.** lion is to mane
- **D.** fish is to fin
- **E.** cat is to fur

23.

Helena has thirty pictures in her photo album. Some of her photos are from a trip to the beach, while others are from her week at summer camp. If she has four times as many photos from the beach as from summer camp, how many beach photos does she have?

    A. 6   **B.** 8   **C.** 18   **D.** 24   **E.** 12

24.

Choose the word that **best** completes this sentence.

When Anna was absent from class, she talked to her teacher, Mr. Jeffries, the next day to find out what she _____.

    A. studied   **B.** learned   **C.** missed   **D.** offered   **E.** read

25.

If the words were arranged to make the best sentence, with which letter would the last word of the sentence begin?

study	decided	library	to	the	at	he

    A. s   **B.** d   **C.** h   **D.** t   **E.** l

26.

A game cannot be played without:

    A. equipment   **B.** fun   **C.** a referee   **D.** a player   **E.** spectators

27.

    What comes next in the series?   4   1   V   1   4   E   4   3   T   3   4   ?

    A. W   **B.** F   **C.** 1   **D.** G   **E.** 7

28.

The drawings below form a series. Which drawing continues that series and goes where you see the question mark?

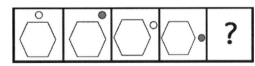

    A   **B**   **C**   **D**   **E**

29.

The numbers in the box go together in a certain way. Which number goes where you see the question mark?

2	10	50
3	15	75
4	20	?

A. 100   **B.** 60   **C.** 90   **D.** 105   **E.** 120

30.

The drawings in the box go together in a certain way. Which drawing goes where you see the question mark?

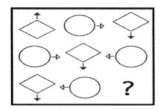

A   B   C   D   E

31.

The numbers in the box go together in a certain way. Which number goes where you see the question mark?

3,4	2,5	2,3,4,5
6,7	?	5,6,7,8

A. 5,8   **B.** 6,8   **C.** 8,5   **D.** 7,8   **E.** 8,6

32.

The opposite of **hate** is:

   A. truth   **B.** dislike   **C.** love   **D.** anger   **E.** loyal

33.

A   B   C   D   E

34.

Andy bought more gum balls than Luke or Dan, but fewer than Caleb. If Andy bought five green gum balls, one blue gum ball, and two red gum balls, then we know for certain that:

    A. Luke bought seven gum balls

    B. Caleb bought at least nine gum balls

    C. Andy likes green gum balls the best

    D. Luke and Dan bought the same number of gum balls

    E. Caleb spent the most money on gum balls

35.

      A   **B**   **C**   **D**   **E**

36.

The numbers in each box go together following the same rule. Figure out that rule and then apply it to the third box. What number goes where you see the question mark?

| 24, 4 | | 36, 6 | | 48, ? | | **A.** 8 | **B.** 6 | **C.** 7 | **D.** 4 | **E.** 12 |

37.

Which word does **not** go with the others?

    A. paintbrush   **B.** pencil   **C.** pen   **D.** crayon   **E.** paper

38.

The numbers in each box go together following the same rule. Figure out that rule and then apply it to the third box. What number goes where you see the question mark?

| 4, 2, 6 | | 5, 3, 9 | | 7, 5, ? | | **A.** 10 | **B.** 15 | **C.** 12 | **D.** 16 | **E.** 11 |

39.

The drawings in the box go together in a certain way. Which drawing goes where you see the question mark?

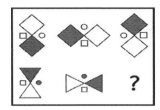

A   B   C   D   E

40.

The numbers in the box go together in a certain way. Which number goes where you see the question mark?

17	25	33
11	19	?

A. 31   **B.** 25   **C.** 27   **D.** 29   **E.** 24

41.

The drawings below form a series. Which drawing continues that series and goes where you see the question mark?

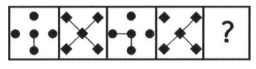

A   B   C   D   E

42.

What number is three less than five times four?

A. 17   **B.** 12   **C.** 5   **D.** 11   **E.** 23

43.

A building isn't a library unless it has:

A. computers   **B.** people   **C.** books   **D.** magazines   **E.** students

44.

Tim, John, and Henry all collect action figures. John has more action figures than Tim or Henry. If John has five action figures, we know for certain that:

A. Tim has zero action figures

B. Tim and Henry both have three action figures

C. All of the boys like to play with action figures

D. Tim and Henry have fewer than five action figures

E. John stole some of Henry's action figures

45.

What comes next in the series?   13   Q   16   S   19   U   22   ?

A. W   B. V   C. 25   D. T   E. 24

46.

 is to as is to:

A   B   C   D   E

47.

If the words were arranged to make the **best** sentence, with which letter would the **third** word of the sentence begin?

| off | do | your | take | not | shoes |

A. o   B. t   C. y   D. s   E. d

48.

The numbers in each box go together following the same rule. Figure out that rule and then apply it to the third box. What number goes where you see the question mark?

12, 9, 9   18, 15, 3   8, 5, ?   A. 10   B. 9   C. 2   D. 6   E. 13

49.

The drawings below form a series. Which drawing continues that series and goes where you see the question mark?

A   B   C   D   E

50.

Choose the word that best completes this sentence.

Halfway home from work, Sarah realized she had _____ her phone and she had to turn back.

   A. remembered   **B.** loaned   **C.** hid   **D.** lost   **E.** forgotten

51.

The drawings in the box go together in a certain way. Which drawing goes where you see the question mark?

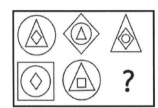

   A   **B**   **C**   **D**   **E**

52.

The numbers in the box go together in a certain way. Which number goes where you see the question mark?

4	10	16
10	16	22
16	22	?

   A. 30   **B.** 6   **C.** 28   **D.** 26   **E.** 32

53.

What comes next in the series?   D   13   F   14   H   15   J   16   L   17   ?

   A. M   **B.** 19   **C.** O   **D.** N   **E.** 18

54.

The words in the box go together in a certain way. Which word goes where you see the question mark?

an	ban	bane
or	?	fore

   A. bore   **B.** more   **C.** flow   **D.** for   **E.** ore

55.

The numbers in each box go together following the same rule. Figure out that rule and then apply it to the third box. What number goes where you see the question mark?

| 9, 3, 5 | 15, 5, 7 | 18, ?, 8 |

A. 9   **B.** 3   **C.** 6   **D.** 7   **E.** 4

56.

Ink is to **pen** as **paint** is to:

A. paper   **B.** brush   **C.** pencil   **D.** watercolor   **E.** painting

57.

Choose the words that **best** complete this sentence.

Don't forget to _____ the letter you _____.

   A. write — found

   B. stamp — received

   C. give — opened

   D. shred — lost

   E. mail — wrote

58.

Marvin's cat just had a litter of nine kittens. Some of the kittens are spotted while the other kittens have stripes. If there are twice as many spotted kittens as striped kittens, how many spotted kittens are there?

   A. 4   **B.** 3   **C.** 6   **D.** 2   **E.** 7

59.

Last week, Elizabeth, Amanda, and Jill all came to school at least one day. Elizabeth was absent from class more than Jill, but not as often as Amanda. If Elizabeth was absent on Monday, Wednesday, and Friday, then we know for certain that:

   A. Each of the three girls skipped school on one of the days they were absent

   B. Jill was absent from class only one day

   C. Amanda was absent on either Tuesday or Thursday

   D. Jill missed Monday or Tuesday

   E. Amanda was present on Tuesday

60.

The opposite of **primitive** is:

    A. simple   **B.** complicated   **C.** modern   **D.** youthful   **E.** ancient

61.

Which word does **not** go with the others?

    A. character   **B.** dialogue   **C.** climax   **D.** plot   **E.** poem

62.

The drawings in the box go together in a certain way. Which drawing goes where you see the question mark?

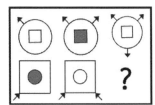

                      A   **B**   **C**   **D**   **E**

63.

If the words were arranged to make the best sentence, with which letter would the last word of the sentence begin?

you	forget	sure	make	don't

    A. m   **B.** f   **C.** s   **D.** y   **E.** d

64.

The numbers in the box go together in a certain way. Which number goes where you see the question mark?

25	16	7
23	14	?

    A. 6   **B.** 5   **C.** 4   **D.** 9   **E.** 8

65.

 is to as is to

                                              A   **B**   **C**   **D**   **E**

66.

Every teacher has:

A. red pens   B. a desk   C. students   D. books   E. a chalkboard

67.

The words in the box go together in a certain way. Which word goes where you see the question mark?

knack	kayak	knock
toast	?	trust

A. think   B. knick   C. tattle   D. king   E. taunt

68.

The numbers in each box go together following the same rule. Figure out that rule and then apply it to the third box. What number goes where you see the question mark?

| 1, 4 | | 2, 8 | | ?, 16 |

A. 3   B. 4   C. 6   D. 2   E. 8

69.

The drawings below form a series. Which drawing continues that series and goes where you see the question mark?

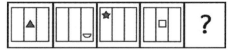 ?

A   B   C   D   E

70.

Slice is to **pizza** as:

A. pasta is to mac and cheese

B. cookie is to milk

C. meat is to meatball

D. bread is to sandwich

E. scoop is to ice cream

71.   **23**

What number comes next in this series?   10   8   15   13   20   18   ?

   A. 16   **B.** 27   **C.** 23   **D.** 20   **E.** 25

72.

What number goes where the question mark is?   8   2   12   3   16   4   20   5   ?   6

   A. 16   **B.** 21   **C.** 19   **D.** 13   **E.** 24

Answer Key

Number	Correct Answer	Type of Question	Number	Correct Answer	Type of Question
1	B	antonym	37	E	verbal classification
2	C	pattern matrix	38	B	number series
3	E	number matrix	39	C	pattern matrix
4	D	verbal classification	40	C	number matrix
5	A	figural series	41	E	figural series
6	B	sentence completion	42	A	arithmetic reasoning
7	D	arithmetic reasoning	43	C	logical selection
8	B	verbal analogy	44	D	inference
9	E	sentence arrangement	45	A	number series
10	B	figural analogy	46	E	figural analogy
11	B	logical selection	47	B	sentence arrangement
12	C	number series	48	E	number series
13	C	figural analogy	49	E	figural series
14	A	verbal classification	50	E	sentence completion
15	B	antonym	51	A	pattern matrix
16	E	pattern matrix	52	C	number matrix
17	D	number matrix	53	D	number series
18	C	word matrix	54	D	word matrix
19	B	number series	55	C	number series
20	D	inference	56	B	verbal analogy
21	B	figural series	57	E	sentence completion
22	A	verbal analogy	58	C	arithmetic reasoning
23	D	arithmetic reasoning	59	C	inference
24	C	sentence completion	60	C	antonym
25	E	sentence arrangement	61	E	verbal classification
26	D	logical selection	62	A	pattern matrix
27	D	number series	63	B	sentence arrangement
28	B	figural series	64	B	number matrix
29	A	number matrix	65	D	figural analogy
30	D	pattern matrix	66	C	logical selection
31	A	number matrix	67	E	word matrix
32	C	antonym	68	B	number series
33	D	figural analogy	69	C	figural series
34	B	inference	70	E	verbal analogy
35	A	figural analogy	71	E	number series
36	A	number series	72	E	number series

Answers Explanations

1. **Correct Answer: B**

   Here, we are looking for the word that can *best* be categorized as the opposite of <u>follow</u>. To follow means to go behind someone or something. Therefore, <u>answer</u>, <u>question</u>, and <u>talk</u> can be eliminated because these words really have nothing to do with the definition of follow. <u>Chase</u> could be a synonym to <u>follow</u>, so it is not the correct answer. The opposite of following is leading, so <u>lead</u> is the correct answer.

2. **Correct Answer: C**

   The pattern in the top row shows that the shaded part of the diamond rotates 90 degrees counterclockwise as we move from left to right. The same pattern applies to the shaded portion of the square in the second row as it also rotates counterclockwise from the first to the second square. Therefore, we need to rotate the shaded area of the second square 90 degrees counterclockwise to find the missing shape, which will also be a square. Answers B and E are immediately eliminated as they are diamonds and not squares. Answer D is wrong because it shows the shaded portion rotated 180 degrees and not 90 as the pattern suggests. Between the squares A and C, the correct answer is C. This is because the shaded part in A is different from the shaded parts of the squares in the second row.

3. **Correct Answer: E**

   The pattern in the first row of the box shows that we are subtracting 7 as we move from left to right (15-7=8 and 8-7=1). The same rule applies on the two first numbers in the second row as we have 19-7=12. Therefore, if we subtract 7 from 12 we will find 5, which is the missing number. Thus, the correct answer is E.

4. **Correct Answer: D**

   Each of the words in this question are items that can be sat upon. Since you cannot sit on a <u>table</u>, option D is the correct answer.

5. **Correct Answer: A**

   In this series, we are given four drawings. Each drawing is comprised of 3 shapes: the innermost shape, the middle shape and the outermost shape. For example, the first drawing is made by the innermost hexagon, the middle circle and the outermost square. Firstly, we need to pay attention to the highlighting of the shapes. We can see that in each drawing, the only shape that is highlighted is either the innermost or the outermost and never the middle one. Specifically, as we move from left to right we have the innermost highlighted shape in the first drawing, then the outermost in the second drawing, then again the innermost in the third drawing and then the outermost in the fourth one. Following this pattern, we expect that the missing drawing must have its innermost shape highlighted and in this way we immediately eliminate choice C. The second thing to note is that, as we progress from left to right, the innermost shape of each drawing becomes the outermost shape for the next drawing: the innermost hexagon in the first drawing is the outermost hexagon of the second drawing, the innermost circle of the second drawing is the outermost circle for the third and the innermost square of the third is the outermost square in the fourth. This pattern guides us to expect the innermost hexagon of the fourth drawing to be the outermost hexagon of the missing drawing. Of the remaining choices, the only one that has a hexagon as the outermost shape is choice A.

6. **Correct Answer: B**

The key to this question is figuring out which set of words works in the blanks. Some answers have one word that may work, but not both. Students must also realize that these words must fill in the blanks so that they complete the cause and effect relationship established in the question. In other words, they must ask themselves: which answer would complete the sentence so that it makes sense why the driver would have to stop? Answer B fulfills this criteria because it makes sense that the driver would have to <u>stop</u> because they were <u>tired.</u> None of the other answer options make sense in this cause-effect context.

7. **Correct Answer: D**

To answer this question, we must first figure out that 3 × 8 = 24. Then, when we add 6, we come up with the answer: 30.

8. **Correct Answer: B**

In this analogy <u>light</u> and <u>dark</u> are opposites. To arrive at the answer, we must figure out the opposite of <u>near,</u> which is <u>far.</u> E is a close answer, but not the *best* answer because <u>near</u> is an adjective, while <u>distance</u> is a noun.

9. **Correct Answer: E**

To solve this problem, students must first correctly arrange the sentence. It should read: "Where have you been all day?" The first word is <u>where,</u> so option E is the correct answer.

10. **Correct Answer: B**

In the first pair of this figural analogy, we can see that both the circle and the square have a diagonal line moving from left to right and they also have two small white shapes (square and circle respectively) underneath them. The second pair must exhibit similar attributes. If we look at the circle of the second pair, we see that it has a diagonal line moving from right to left with the small square now being on top of it and highlighted. Therefore, we need to find in the given choices a square which has a diagonal going in the same direction (right to left) and has a small highlighted circle on top of it. The correct answer is therefore choice B.

11. **Correct Answer: B**

The key to this question is realizing that to actually *sing* a song, a person must be singing *words*, and so <u>lyrics</u> is the correct answer. Though <u>music, instruments, an audience,</u> and <u>a band</u> all relate to music, a song can still be a song without each of these things.

12. **Correct Answer: C**

The key observation here, is that if we break up this series into pairs of numbers, we will have four pairs (31,27 29,27 ?,27 and 25,27) where the second number is always 27 and the first number is decreasing by 2 starting from 31. Since the missing number is the first number of the third pair, it must be 31-2-2=27. Therefore, the correct answer is C.

13. **Correct Answer: C**

In the first pair of this figural analogy, we can notice the following: a) both shapes are the same (circles with small squares). b) the position of the small square switches from the left of the first circle to the bottom of the second one. c) the highlighting alternates for both the circle and the square. Similar traits must be applied to the second pair which has a non-highlighted triangle with a small highlighted circle on its left. Thus, we are looking for the same shape (triangle with a small circle), with the circle being located to the bottom and with alternated highlighting (highlighted triangle with a non-highlighted circle). Choices A and D are eliminated as they have the circle on top and on the right side of the triangle. Choice E is eliminated because the triangle is not highlighted. Choice B is also eliminated because the circle is highlighted but should not be. Therefore, choice C is correct.

14. **Correct Answer: A**

Here, we are looking for the words that does *not* belong with the others. Each of the words here is a synonym for "eat." <u>Consume</u>, <u>eat</u>, <u>ingest</u>, and <u>devour</u> are all synonyms. The correct answer is <u>digest</u> because, thought it does have to do with the process of eating food, it doesn't actually mean "to eat." Students might think of it as the phase *after* eating something.

15. **Correct Answer: B**

Here, we are looking for the opposite of <u>truth</u>. <u>Hope</u> and <u>healing</u> don't have anything to do with the definition of this word, so they are incorrect. While <u>history</u> might be considered a type of truth, it is not its antonym. <u>Fact</u> is a synonym of <u>truth</u>. The correct answer, then, is fiction. Since fiction is something that is made up, it is the opposite of <u>truth</u>.

16. **Correct Answer: E**

In the top row, we can see the following relationships between the first two circles: a) the diagonal line changes direction (from left to right in the first circle, to right to left in the second one). b) the small arrow changes position (from the top of the first circle to the bottom of the second circle) and c) the highlighting of the small arrow alternates (from non-highlighted in the first circle to highlighted in the second one). The third circle has all the traits of the previous two combined: the two diagonal lines and the two small arrows in their positions with their highlighting again alternated (now neither are highlighted). This pattern must be applied in the second row to find the second square. Firstly, we eliminate choice C as it is a circle and not a square. Then, we note that the first square in the second row has a diagonal that goes from right to left, so we are looking for a square with a left to right diagonal. Choices A and B do not exhibit this so they can be eliminated. The first square has also a small highlighted circle on the bottom, so we need to find a square with a non-highlighted circle on top. Between the two remaining choices D and E, only E has the non-highlighted small circle on top, so E is the correct choice.

17. **Correct Answer: D**

The pattern in the first and second row of the box shows that as we move from left to right we multiply the numbers by 3 (2×3=6 and 6×3=18 for the first row and 3×3=9 and 9×3=27 for the second row). Therefore, the missing number is 4×3=12 which is also validated by the next number 36 as 12×3=36. Therefore, the correct answer is D.

18. **Correct Answer: C**

In this matrix, the words in the top row all begin with the same first *two* letters: <u>fl</u>. This means that the words in the second row should each begin with the same two letters. Since the second and third words in this row begin with <u>an</u>, we can conclude that the word needed to replace the question mark should begin this way as well, so <u>angle</u> is the correct answer.

19. **Correct Answer: B**

The pattern in the first two boxes shows that the second number is the quotient of the first when divided by 4 (12/4=3 and 16/4=4). Therefore, the correct answer is B as 20/4=5.

20. **Correct Answer: D**

With this question, students must reason through some of the answers. We can immediately eliminate option B because it is subjective; there is no indication that the reason Olivia gave up her tickets is because of generosity. We also don't know how many tickets Sofie began with, so we can eliminate options C and E. What we do know is that Carlos bought the most tickets, so the number he purchased must be at least greater than 15; this is because we know that Olivia has at least 15 tickets, but we don't know if Sophie had any tickets to begin with at all.

21. **Correct Answer: B**

In this series, we have four drawings. Each drawing is made up of an inner and an outer shape. Each inner shape always has an arrow attached which rotates counter-clockwise as we move from left to right: from the top to the left, then down and then to the right in the fourth drawing. Therefore, we expect that the missing shape will be one with an arrow attached on the top of its inner shape. Based on this, we can eliminate A, C and D because in choices A and C the arrow is attached on the bottom of the inner shape, while in choice D it is attached on the top of the outer and not the inner shape as it should be. To make our final selection among B and E, we observe that the outer shapes of the given four drawings in this series are all different to each other: circle, square, hexagon and triangle. Therefore, the missing drawing must be one with a new different outer shape, which is the diamond in choice B.

22. **Correct Answer: A**

In this question, the key is to pay attention to the relationship between the words in the analogy. When solving an analogy, it is helpful to put the words being compared into a sentence, as in this case: a <u>tiger's</u> fur has <u>stripes</u>. The only answer options that would fit into this answer format is option A. A dalmatian's fur has spots. Answer options B does relate to the how the polar bear's fur looks; however, unlike a dalmatian's spots or tiger's stripes, it does not describe a pattern of fur, just a color. Therefore it is in correct. Answers C, D, and E all relate to something an animal has: a cat has fur, a fish has fins, and a lion has a mane. However, none of these answer options relate to the pattern of an animal's fur.

23. **Correct Answer: D**

There are a number of ways to solve this problem. In working through this answer, students will need to observe that the question requires figuring out that 30 must be divided by a factor of 5 (4 parts beach photos, 1 part summer camp). Or, students might observe that they are dealing with a 4 to 1 ratio. Either way, students must figure out that the number of camp photos is 6, while the number of beach photos is 24.

24. Correct Answer: C

In this sentence, the context clue is <u>Anna was absent from class</u>. Students should be able to conclude that, if absent, Anna would probably want to find out what she <u>missed</u>. <u>Studied</u>, <u>learned</u>, and <u>read</u> may have all been things she missed out on doing in class, but they do not work in the blank provide**d.**

25. Correct Answer: E

In this question, students will of course have to make the words provided into a co-herent sentence first. The sentence should be "He decided to study at the library." Since the last word of the sentence is <u>library</u>, the answer is <u>E</u>.

26. Correct Answer: D

By definition, a game cannot be played unless there is a <u>player</u> to play it. Though many games require an <u>equipment</u>, a <u>referee</u>, or <u>spectators</u>, these things are not vital to all games. Additionally, fun is something subjective, so we can't say its necessary to have fun to make a game.

27. Correct Answer: D

The first thing we can observe in this series of numbers and letters is that each pair of numbers is followed by a letter as we go from left to right. The first pair 4 1 is followed by V, the second pair 1 4 is followed by E and so on. Since we are looking for what comes after the 3 4 pair, we understand that this should be a letter. Thus, we immedi-ately eliminate choices C and E, which are numbers. Now, in order to find which letter goes where the question mark is, we need to reveal the relationship between the num-bers and the letters. The key to this question is to understand the triple 1 4 E. We ob-serve that the sum of 1 and 4 is 5 and E is the 5th letter of the alphabet (A, B, C, D, E). If we move to the triple 4 1 V, we also see that the sum of 4 and 1 is again 5 and V is the 5th letter of the alphabet when we count backwards starting from Z (Z, Y, X, W, V). The same for group 4 3 T where 4+3 = 7 and T is the 7th letter counting backwards the al-phabet (Z, Y, X, W, V, U, T). Therefore, the pair 3 4 which sums up to 7 must be followed by the 7th letter of the alphabet which is G (A, B, C, D, E, F, G). The correct answer is D.

28. Correct Answer: B

In the first drawing of this series, we see a hexagon with a small circle located right above the middle point of the top side. As we progress from left to right, we see the small circle moving clockwise and passing through every vertex and middle point of every side. It also alternates its highlighting in each step. Since the fourth hexagon has the circle just next to its vertex on the right and the circle is highlighted, the next hexagon will have a non-highlighted circle located outside the bottom right side and just next to its middle point. Therefore, the correct answer is B.

29. Correct Answer: A

The pattern in the first and second rows of the box shows that as we move from left to right we multiply the numbers by 5. (2×5=10 and 10×5=50 for the first row and 3×5=15 and 15×5=75 for the second row). Since the same rule applies for the first two numbers in the third row (4×5=20), it is implied that the missing number will be the outcome of 20 times 5, which is 100. Therefore, the Choice A is correct.

30.   Correct Answer: D

In this pattern matrix, we see a series of drawings in each row in which the shape alternates between diamond and circle, and the arrow rotates 90 degrees clockwise. At the same time, the arrow alternates between highlighted and not highlighted. Since the drawing in the third row before the question mark is a circle, we know we are looking for a diamond. Therefore, we can eliminate choices B and E. Also, the drawing in the final row before the question mark has an arrow pointing to the left with no highlighting, so we know we need to find a drawing among the answer options which has an arrow pointing upwards (because the arrow will be rotated 90 degrees clockwise). Therefore, choice A is eliminated. Finally, we want that arrow to be highlighted as the arrow of the drawing before the question mark is not highlighted. Therefore the drawing we are looking for is a diamond with the highlighted arrow pointing up. That drawing is shown in D.

31.   Correct Answer: A

In the first row, we need to identify the relationship between the two pairs of numbers and the series of four numbers in the end. We can see that the four number series is created by placing the first pair of numbers in between the two numbers of the second pair. (We take both 3,4 of the first pair and locate them in the same order between the 2 and 5 of the second pair). So, the first and fourth number of the four number series represent the second pair in the first row (in the same order). This same pattern must be applied to the second row. Therefore, first and fourth number in the four number series, 5 and 8, must represent the pair of numbers we are looking for. Therefore, the correct answer is A.

32.   Correct Answer: C

Love is the correct answer because it is the *best* opposite of hate. Both love and hate are extremes, so the word dislike is not strong enough to be a true antonym.

33.   Correct Answer: D

In the first pair of this figural analogy, we see that the shape of the two combined triangles remains the same while the small circle alternates between two opposite (left-right) positions. The highlighting of the circle also alternates from not shaded to shaded. The similar pattern must be applied to the second pair. The first drawing is a square with a horizontal line across it and a highlighted triangle on its bottom side. So, we initially need to find the same shape (square with a horizontal line) among the answer options which means that choices A and C are eliminated. Now, we want a square to have its triangle in the opposite position and with alternated shading (thus with no shading). The drawing with the unshaded triangle on the top side of the square is the drawing that fits. Therefore, choice D is correct.

34.   Correct Answer: B

In this question, students can eliminate options B and E right away because both of these answer are based on assumptions but not on any information provided in the question. In particular, for option E, just because Caleb bought the most doesn't mean he spent the most money—we don't know anything about the pricing of the gum balls. The question also does not mention anything about Luke and Dan buying the same number of gum balls; it is possible, but not certain, so <u>D</u> cannot be correct. Similarly, <u>A</u> is incorrect because we can't come to any conclusion about how many gum balls Luke bought.

35. Correct Answer: A

In the first pair of this figural analogy, we note the following: a) the group of four identical shapes stacked on two rows becomes a group of three identical new shapes, stacked again on two rows, with the single shape being in the top row (four circles change to three triangles with one triangle in the top row) b) the highlighting of the rows alternates (the group of four circles has its bottom row highlighted, while the group of three triangles has its top row highlighted). The same pattern must be applied to the second pair too, which has as a first element a group of four triangles stacked on two rows with the top row highlighted. This means that we are looking for a group of three new shapes (circles) which means that anything related to triangles should be eliminated (choices B and E). We can also eliminate choice D as it represents four circles and not three as the pattern suggests. The final part is to identify the drawing with the correct highlighting, which needs to alternate. That means we need the bottom row to be highlighted (as the group of four triangles has its top row highlighted). Therefore, the correct answer is A.

36. Correct Answer: A

The pattern in the first two boxes shows that the second number is the quotient of the division of the first one by 6 (24/6=4 and 36/6=6). Therefore, 48/6=8 and the correct answer is A.

37. Correct Answer: E

In this series, each of these words is something than can be used to write or mark with paper— they are all tools. However, paper is the only item on this list that isn't a tool for the process of writing or drawing.

38. Correct Answer: B

The key observation here is that the two first numbers in each box differ by 2. This means that if we subtract 2 from the first number we get the second number (4−2=2, 5−2=3, 7−2=5). Now, the second number in each of the first two boxes leads us to the third number by multiplying it by 3 (2×3=6 and 3×3=9). Therefore, we have to multiply the second number in the third box by 3 to find the missing number, which is 5×3=15. Thus, the correct answer is B.

39. Correct Answer: C

Each figure in the first row of this pattern matrix is comprised of two connected diamonds with a small square and a small circle next to the connection point on both sides. If we rotate the first figure 90 degrees clockwise, the second figure is similar to the first except that the small circle and square are in opposite positions. We see the same pattern when we rotate the second figure by 90 degrees clockwise. We get a shape similar to the third figure except for the two small shapes which are in opposite positions. This leads us to think that the pattern must be "rotate by 90 degrees clockwise and switch the positions of the small circle and square each time you rotate". This pattern indeed describes the positions of the figures as we move from left to right. And this pattern applies to the second row too, as we can see from the first two figures. The first figure is a pair of two connected triangles with a small square and a small circle next to the connection point on both sides. The second figure is the first one rotated by 90 degrees clockwise, but with the positions of the circle and square switched. So, if we apply the rule to the second figure we will find the missing third one. By rotating the second figure by 90 degrees clockwise, we will get a shape with a highlighted bottom triangle. Thus, choices A, D and E are eliminated as the first two are connected diamonds and not triangles and the third one has its top triangle highlighted instead of the bottom one. Now we need to figure out what the positions of the square and circle will be. Before the rotation of the second figure, the circle was up and the square was down. After the rotation by 90 degrees clockwise, the circle will be on the right and the square on the left. But the shapes will also need to change positions, so to end up with a circle on the left and a square on the right. Both B and C are those types of shapes, however, B is the result of rotating, switching positions and alternating the highlighting between the circle and the square, which is not the case in this pattern. Both circle and square must maintain the highlighting pattern of the two previous drawings (non-highlighted square, highlighted circle). Thus, the correct answer is C.

40. Correct Answer: C

The pattern in the first row of the box shows that we are adding 8 as we move from left to right (15+8=25 and 25+8=33). The same rule applies to the first two numbers in the second row as 11+8=19. Therefore, to find the right answer we need to add 8 to 19 and we'll get 27. The correct answer is C.

41. Correct Answer: E

In this series, a group of five **dots** and a group of five **diamonds** alternate as we move from left to right. Since the fourth figure contains diamonds, we understand that the missing figure will contain dots. Thus, choices A and D are eliminated. We can now see that the first figure has 2 of its dots connected forming 1 line segment. The second figure has all 5 diamonds connected forming 4 line segments. As we move to the third figure with the dots, we can see that now we have 2 line segments, one more than the first drawing. The fourth figure with the diamonds has 3 line segments, one less than the second drawing. Therefore, the pattern here is that, as we move from left to right, the line segments formed by the dots increase by one while the line segments formed by the diamonds decrease by one. Therefore, since the last drawing with dots (the third one) has 2 line segments, we expect that the missing figure will have one more line segment formed (3). Among the three remaining choices, B, C and E, only choice E has 3 line segments. Choice B has 4 line segments and choice C has 2 line segments. Therefore, the correct answer is E.

42. Correct Answer: A

To answer this question, we first have to figure out that 5 × 4 = 20. When we subtract 3, we then get 17.

43. Correct Answer: C

By definition, a library is a building that houses <u>books</u>. Though a library may have all of the other answer options inside its walls—<u>computers</u>, <u>people</u>, <u>magazines</u>, and <u>students</u>— these are not the things which make a library a library.

44. Correct Answer: D

After reading this question, we know for certain that, because John has five action figures and because Tim and Henry have less than him, this must mean that Tim and Henry have fewer than five action figures. Though answer options A and B are possible, we cannot be certain based on the information given. Additionally, C and E are based on assumptions but not on information in the question, so these are also incorrect.

45. Correct Answer: A

Immediately, we see that every 2-digit number is followed by a letter. Since the question mark follows a number, we conclude that we are looking for a letter. Thus, choices C and E can be eliminated. Now, if we take a closer look at how the letters progress, we'll see that starting from Q we skip one letter and go to the next one as shown in the below pattern:

Q R S T U V W ....

Thus, the missing letter is W, and choice A is correct.

46. Correct Answer: E

The first pair of this figural analogy is comprised of two big identical shapes (hexagons), which include different small shapes (triangle and circle). Both big and small shapes have alternated shading. The same pattern must be applied to the second pair, which has a shaded triangle with a non-shaded square in it. Therefore, the missing drawing must have the same unshaded shape (triangle) as the outermost shape, with a shaded shape inside other than square. A, B and C choices can be eliminated because they are not triangles. Although both D and E have unshaded triangles, and include a diamond, only E has a shaded diamond. Therefore, the correct answer is E.

47. Correct Answer: B

To answer this question, a student must first arrange the sentence. If a student can identify a pairing between "do" and "not" and "take" and "off", then a logical sentence can become clear from the words in the box: "Do not take off your shoes". The third word of the sentence starts with the letter "t". So, option B is the correct answer.

48. Correct Answer: E

By taking the first two numbers in each box, we see that they differ by 3. This means that if we subtract 3 from the first number we get the second number (12−3=9, 18−3=15 and 8−3=5). This is the first rule that leads us from the first number to the second one in each box. Now, we need to identify which rule guides us to the third number. This is the tricky part of this problem as there is no obvious clue on how to progress. However if we take a closer look at the second and third numbers of the first two boxes, we can see that when they are added together they give the same result (9+9=18 and 15+3=18). This means that the third number is 18 minus the second number. If we apply this new rule to the third box, we see that 18−5=13. Therefore, the correct answer is E.

49. Correct Answer: E

In this series, the number of shaded squares increase by 2 as we progress from left to right. They also alternate their direction (horizontal, vertical, horizontal and again vertical). Since the fourth drawing has 8 shaded squares vertically aligned, we can expect the missing drawing to have 10 shaded squares aligned horizontally. Choices A and D have 12 and 8 shaded squares respectively, so they can be eliminated. Among the remaining choices, only E has the 10 shaded squares aligned horizontally. Thus, choice E is the correct answer.

50. Correct Answer: E

Here, the context clue provided is the phrase <u>she had to turn back</u>. Students must then decide which of these answer options, if filled in the blank, would provide a reason that Sarah would have to go back to work. Students may be tempted to choose answer D; however, there is nothing in the sentence to indicate her phone is <u>lost</u>. While Sarah did <u>remember</u> she forgot her phone, this word doesn't work in the given blank either. <u>Forgotten</u> should be used to fill in the blank because this provides a reason that Sarah might go back to work.

51. Correct Answer: A

In the top row of this pattern matrix, we see that each drawing is comprised of 3 shapes: the innermost shape, the middle shape and the outermost shape. For example, the first drawing is made by a diamond as the innermost shape, a triangle as the middle shape and the circle as the outermost shape. By examining how the pattern of the top row progresses as we move from left to right, we can see that the innermost shape of each drawing becomes the outermost shape of the next drawing. (The innermost diamond in the first drawing becomes the outermost shape of the second drawing and the innermost triangle in the second drawing becomes the outermost shape of the third one). However, this is <u>not</u> the case for the bottom row. As we can see, the innermost diamond in the first drawing is nowhere in the second. Therefore, we need to find another pattern that applies to this matrix before we answer correctly. Another observation is that, in each row, all the outermost, middle and innermost shapes are different (for example in the first, second and third drawing of the first row we have circle, diamond, triangle as outermost shapes, triangle, circle, diamond as middle shapes and diamond, triangle and circle as innermost ones respectively). The same rule needs to be applied in the second row, therefore we need to find a drawing that has different outermost, middle and innermost shapes than the other two in the bottom row. Choices B, C and D can be eliminated as they all have outermost shapes that already exist in the row (circle or square). Between the two triangles in choices A and E, the one in E has the same middle shape as the first drawing of the bottom row (circle). Therefore, the correct answer is A. This drawing has a different outermost, middle and innermost shapes than the other two drawings in the row.

52. Correct Answer: C

The pattern in this matrix is that we add 6 to each number to find the next one in the same row (4+6=10, 10+6=16 for the first row, 10+6=16, 16+6=22 for the second one and 16+6=22 for the third row). Therefore, by adding 6 to 22 we find 28. This is the missing number of the third row. So, the correct answer is C.

53. Correct Answer: D

In this series, letters and two-digit numbers alternate, with 17 being the last number just before the question mark. This means that the missing term that follows must be a letter. Therefore, we can eliminate choices B and E, which are numbers. If we separate the numbers from letters, we see that while the numbers grow by 1, the letters progress by skipping every other letter starting from D. Therefore, the letter that comes after L must be N. The correct answer is choice D.

54. **Correct Answer: D**

In order to answer this question, students must observe the pattern in the top row. Moving from <u>an</u> to <u>ban,</u> one letter has been added at to the beginning of the word. Moving from <u>ban</u> to <u>bane</u>, one letter has been added at the end. Using this same pattern, we can conclude that the word needed to replace the question mark should be the word in the third column minus one letter at the beginning. So, the answer is <u>for</u>. Students might tempted to choose the word <u>ore</u>, as this is also a three-letter word; however, moving from <u>or</u> to <u>ore</u> requires adding a letter at the end of <u>or</u>, not the beginning.

55. **Correct Answer: C**

In the first two boxes, we see that the division of the first number by 3 gives the second number (9/3=3 and 15/3=5). Then, we need to add 2 to the second number to get the third one (3+2=5 and 5+2=7). By applying this rule to the third box, we get 18/3=6 which gives us 8 when increased by 2. Therefore, the missing number is 6 and the correct answer is C.

56. **Correct Answer: B**

For this analogy, we can figure out the answer by discovering the relationship between the words. A <u>pen</u> uses <u>ink</u> to mark on paper, while a <u>brush</u> uses <u>paint</u> to mark on paper.

57. **Correct Answer: E**

For this question, the key is figuring out which answer options contains words which will *both* work in the context of the sentence. The only answer with two words fit clearly in the blanks is E.

58. **Correct Answer: C**

With this question, we have to figure out that the ratio of spotted kittens to striped kittens is 2:1. Taking into consideration that there are 9 kittens total, we can conclude that there are 6 spotted kittens and 3 striped kittens.

59. **Correct Answer: C**

In working through this problem, students can eliminate answer <u>A</u> because it is a mere assumption based on the information provided; the question says nothing about skipping school, so this is not the best answer. Students will also need to realize that Amanda was absent more days than Elizabeth. This means that Amanda must have been absent at least four weekdays, so she only came to school one day of the week. We can conclude that one of the days she missed must have been either Tuesday or Thursday, so option C is correct. We can conclude no information about Jill because we only know that she was absent fewer days than Elizabeth; however, this means Jill could have been absent one or two days. Additionally, we do not have any information about the days which Jill missed.

60. Correct Answer: C

Something that is <u>primitive</u> relates to an early stage of development; therefore, <u>modern</u> is the best antonym. While something that is <u>primitive</u> may be <u>simple</u>, this is not necessarily an opposite.

61. Correct Answer: E

In this question, most of the answer options relate to something in a story: <u>character</u>, <u>dialogue</u>, <u>climax</u>, and <u>plot</u>. A <u>poem</u>, though it is a type of writing, is not a part of a story, so it does not fit here.

62. Correct Answer: A

In the first row of this matrix, we have circles with small squares inside them and some arrows attached pointing outside the circle. As we move from left to right, the highlighting of the square alternates and the arrows increase by 1, keeping their direction of pointing outside, with a total of 3 in the last drawing. Also, we note that the first drawing has a single arrow on the top of the circle, the second drawing has two arrows on the top of the circle, and the third drawing has a third arrow at the bottom of the circle in a vertical direction. This pattern must be applied to the second row, where we have squares with small circles inside that have alternated highlighting. In each of the drawings, there is an arrow (or two) attached to the bottom sides of the squares pointing towards the inside. Since the second square of this row has a non-highlighted circle inside, the missing figure will be a square with a highlighted circle inside. Therefore, choices C and E can be eliminated. Moreover, given that the two arrows are at the bottom of the square pointing inside, the missing figure will have a third arrow on top of the square also pointing inside. Therefore, choice C is eliminated as the top arrow is pointing in the opposite direction. Finally, we want the arrow on top to be in a vertical direction as in the third drawing of the top row of the matrix, so choice B is eliminated as the arrow on top has a diagonal direction. Therefore, the correct answer is A.

63. Correct Answer: B

To answer this question, we must first make a complete sentence from the words provided. The sentence should read "Make sure you don't forget." Since the last word is <u>forget</u>, the correct answer is B.

64. Correct Answer: B

The pattern in this matrix is that we subtract 9 from each number to find the next one in the same row (25−9=16 and 16−9=7 for the first row, and 23−9=14 for the second row). Therefore, by subtracting 9 from 14, we find 5, which is the missing number. So, the correct answer is B.

65. Correct Answer: D

The first pair of this figural analogy has two hexagons partitioned into six equal parts each. As we observe the two hexagons, we can see that the second hexagon is created when we alternate the shading of the first one and then rotate it counterclockwise by one part. Like the first pair which has two hexagons, the second pair will also be comprised of two circles. Thus, choice B is eliminated because it is a hexagon. Now we can see that the circle of the second pair is also partitioned into 6 equal parts with one of its parts shaded. This means that if we change the shading according to the pattern, this shaded piece will not have shading and all other five will be shaded. Therefore, we can also eliminate choice C, which has two pieces without shading. Now, if we rotate this circle counterclockwise by one part, this non-shaded piece will be found exactly at the bottom of the circle. This means that we can eliminate choices A and E, which have non-shaded pieces on the left of the circle (top-left and bottom-left respectively). Therefore, the correct answer is D.

66. **Correct Answer: C**

Though many teachers will have <u>red pens</u>, a <u>desk</u>, <u>books</u>, and a <u>chalkboard</u>, we cannot say definitively that *every* teacher will have these things. Of the answer choices provided, we can only say that every teacher will have <u>students</u>.

67. **Correct Answer: E**

For this word matrix, the words in the top row all begin and end with the letter k. They are also all five letters in length. In the second row, this means that all words must start with the same letter and and be the same number of letters. Each word in the second row, then, must start and end with <u>t</u> and be five letters in length. Therefore, <u>taunt</u> is the correct answer.

68. **Correct Answer: B**

The rule here is that in each box we must multiply the first number by 4 to get the second one (1×4=4 and 2×4=8). Or, equivalently, if we divide the second number by 4 we will get the first one (4/1=1 and 8/4=2). So, by dividing the second number in the third box by 4 we will find the missing number (16/4=4). Therefore, the correct answer is B.

69. **Correct Answer: C**

In this series, each square is partitioned into three columns where one column includes a small shape. As we move from left to right, we find the small shapes in different columns with the following pattern: middle column, right column, left column and again middle column. Given that the fourth square has the small shape in its middle column, we can conclude that the missing square will have the small shape in the column on the right. Thus, we can eliminate choices B and E as the drawings have small shapes in the left and middle column respectively. We can also note that as we move from left to right, the position of the small shape within a column varies according to the following pattern: middle of the column, bottom of the column, top of the column, and again middle of the column. Therefore, as the fourth square has the small shape in the middle of the column, the missing square will have a shape at the bottom of the relative column. That means we can also eliminate choice D because it is at the top of the column. Finally, we see that the shading of the small shapes alternates as we progress from left to right. Since the fourth square has a shape that is not shaded, the missing square must have a shaded one. Therefore, the correct answer is C.

70. **Correct answer: E**

The key with this question to make the analogy into a sentence; this makes it easier to discern the answer. We could say for this question "a <u>slice</u> is a serving of <u>pizza</u>." So then, the only answer option that would work is <u>E</u> because a <u>scoop</u> is a serving of <u>ice cream</u>. Some of the other answer options are a part of a whole, rather than a serving: meat is part of a meatball, bread is part of a sandwich, and pasta is part of mac and cheese. A cookie goes with milk, but it is not a serving.

71. **Correct Answer: E**

The pattern here is that as we move from left to right, we alternate subtracting 2 and adding 7 as shown below:

$$10 \ (-2) \ 8 \ (+7) \ 15 \ (-2) \ 13 \ (+7) \ 20 \ (-2) \ 18$$

Thus, we need to add 7 to 18 to find the missing number which is 18+7=25. So the correct answer is E.

72. **Correct Answer: E**

The pattern here is that we are dividing every other number by 4, and then adding to the quotient a progressively increasing by 3 number, as shown below:

$$8 \ (/4) \ 2 \ (+10) \ 12 \ (/4) \ 3 \ (+13) \ 16 \ (/4) \ 4 \ (+16) \ 20 \ (/4) \ 5 \ (+19) \ 24 \ (/4) \ 6$$

As we see, the number 24 should be where the questions mark is. Therefore the correct answer is E.

Origins Publications

Name: _____   Date: _____

1. Ⓐ Ⓑ Ⓒ Ⓓ Ⓔ   19. Ⓐ Ⓑ Ⓒ Ⓓ Ⓔ   37. Ⓐ Ⓑ Ⓒ Ⓓ Ⓔ   55. Ⓐ Ⓑ Ⓒ Ⓓ Ⓔ

2. Ⓐ Ⓑ Ⓒ Ⓓ Ⓔ   20. Ⓐ Ⓑ Ⓒ Ⓓ Ⓔ   38. Ⓐ Ⓑ Ⓒ Ⓓ Ⓔ   56. Ⓐ Ⓑ Ⓒ Ⓓ Ⓔ

3. Ⓐ Ⓑ Ⓒ Ⓓ Ⓔ   21. Ⓐ Ⓑ Ⓒ Ⓓ Ⓔ   39. Ⓐ Ⓑ Ⓒ Ⓓ Ⓔ   57. Ⓐ Ⓑ Ⓒ Ⓓ Ⓔ

4. Ⓐ Ⓑ Ⓒ Ⓓ Ⓔ   22. Ⓐ Ⓑ Ⓒ Ⓓ Ⓔ   40. Ⓐ Ⓑ Ⓒ Ⓓ Ⓔ   58. Ⓐ Ⓑ Ⓒ Ⓓ Ⓔ

5. Ⓐ Ⓑ Ⓒ Ⓓ Ⓔ   23. Ⓐ Ⓑ Ⓒ Ⓓ Ⓔ   41. Ⓐ Ⓑ Ⓒ Ⓓ Ⓔ   59. Ⓐ Ⓑ Ⓒ Ⓓ Ⓔ

6. Ⓐ Ⓑ Ⓒ Ⓓ Ⓔ   24. Ⓐ Ⓑ Ⓒ Ⓓ Ⓔ   42. Ⓐ Ⓑ Ⓒ Ⓓ Ⓔ   60. Ⓐ Ⓑ Ⓒ Ⓓ Ⓔ

7. Ⓐ Ⓑ Ⓒ Ⓓ Ⓔ   25. Ⓐ Ⓑ Ⓒ Ⓓ Ⓔ   43. Ⓐ Ⓑ Ⓒ Ⓓ Ⓔ   61. Ⓐ Ⓑ Ⓒ Ⓓ Ⓔ

8. Ⓐ Ⓑ Ⓒ Ⓓ Ⓔ   26. Ⓐ Ⓑ Ⓒ Ⓓ Ⓔ   44. Ⓐ Ⓑ Ⓒ Ⓓ Ⓔ   62. Ⓐ Ⓑ Ⓒ Ⓓ Ⓔ

9. Ⓐ Ⓑ Ⓒ Ⓓ Ⓔ   27. Ⓐ Ⓑ Ⓒ Ⓓ Ⓔ   45. Ⓐ Ⓑ Ⓒ Ⓓ Ⓔ   63. Ⓐ Ⓑ Ⓒ Ⓓ Ⓔ

10. Ⓐ Ⓑ Ⓒ Ⓓ Ⓔ   28. Ⓐ Ⓑ Ⓒ Ⓓ Ⓔ   46. Ⓐ Ⓑ Ⓒ Ⓓ Ⓔ   64. Ⓐ Ⓑ Ⓒ Ⓓ Ⓔ

11. Ⓐ Ⓑ Ⓒ Ⓓ Ⓔ   29. Ⓐ Ⓑ Ⓒ Ⓓ Ⓔ   47. Ⓐ Ⓑ Ⓒ Ⓓ Ⓔ   65. Ⓐ Ⓑ Ⓒ Ⓓ Ⓔ

12. Ⓐ Ⓑ Ⓒ Ⓓ Ⓔ   30. Ⓐ Ⓑ Ⓒ Ⓓ Ⓔ   48. Ⓐ Ⓑ Ⓒ Ⓓ Ⓔ   66. Ⓐ Ⓑ Ⓒ Ⓓ Ⓔ

13. Ⓐ Ⓑ Ⓒ Ⓓ Ⓔ   31. Ⓐ Ⓑ Ⓒ Ⓓ Ⓔ   49. Ⓐ Ⓑ Ⓒ Ⓓ Ⓔ   67. Ⓐ Ⓑ Ⓒ Ⓓ Ⓔ

14. Ⓐ Ⓑ Ⓒ Ⓓ Ⓔ   32. Ⓐ Ⓑ Ⓒ Ⓓ Ⓔ   50. Ⓐ Ⓑ Ⓒ Ⓓ Ⓔ   68. Ⓐ Ⓑ Ⓒ Ⓓ Ⓔ

15. Ⓐ Ⓑ Ⓒ Ⓓ Ⓔ   33. Ⓐ Ⓑ Ⓒ Ⓓ Ⓔ   51. Ⓐ Ⓑ Ⓒ Ⓓ Ⓔ   69. Ⓐ Ⓑ Ⓒ Ⓓ Ⓔ

16. Ⓐ Ⓑ Ⓒ Ⓓ Ⓔ   34. Ⓐ Ⓑ Ⓒ Ⓓ Ⓔ   52. Ⓐ Ⓑ Ⓒ Ⓓ Ⓔ   70. Ⓐ Ⓑ Ⓒ Ⓓ Ⓔ

17. Ⓐ Ⓑ Ⓒ Ⓓ Ⓔ   35. Ⓐ Ⓑ Ⓒ Ⓓ Ⓔ   53. Ⓐ Ⓑ Ⓒ Ⓓ Ⓔ   71. Ⓐ Ⓑ Ⓒ Ⓓ Ⓔ

18. Ⓐ Ⓑ Ⓒ Ⓓ Ⓔ   36. Ⓐ Ⓑ Ⓒ Ⓓ Ⓔ   54. Ⓐ Ⓑ Ⓒ Ⓓ Ⓔ   72. Ⓐ Ⓑ Ⓒ Ⓓ Ⓔ

OLSAT© Level E
Practice Test 2

1.

The opposite of **novice** is:

A. beginner   **B.** know-it-all   **C.** intermediate   **D.** professional   **E.** expert

2.

The drawings in the box go together in a certain way. Which drawing goes where you see the question mark?

3.

Page is to **book** as **brick** is to:

A. building   **B.** concrete   **C.** hard   **D.** heavy   **E.** fire

4.

The drawings below form a series. Which drawing completes that series and goes where you see the question mark?

5.

Homes always have:

A. two stories   **B.** several rooms   **C.** beds   **D.** inhabitants   **E.** pets

6.

You probably _____ the test because you didn't _____ the material.

A. passed — study

B. failed — read

C. wrote — like

D. questioned — forgot

E. aced — understand

7.

Which word does **not** go with the others?

A. shine   **B.** shackles   **C.** shirts   **D.** shades   **E.** shakes

8.

Liza is older than Madison, but younger than Tiffany. We know for certain that:

A. Tiffany is the most mature.

B. The three are sisters.

C. Tiffany is the eldest.

D. Liza and Madison are two years apart.

E. Tiffany is older by at least three years.

9.

 is to as is to:

A   **B**   **C**   **D**   **E**

10.

If the words were arranged to make the **best** sentence, with which letter would the **second** word of the sentence begin?

mine	hand	your	put	in

A. p   **B.** y   **C.** h   **D.** i   **E.** m

11.

Note is to **scale** as:

A. Star is to constellation.

B. Book is to chapter.

C. Singer is to album.

D. Ink is to paper.

E. Recipe is to meal.

12.

The words in the box go together in a certain way. Which word goes where you see the question mark?

on	son	song
an	?	mane

A. ant   **B.** san   **C.** man   **D.** ton   **E.** ban

13.

The drawings below form a series. Which drawing continues that series and goes where you see the question mark?

A   B   C   D   E

14.

Be sure to _____ the dishes that were _____ during the dinner.

A. wash — dirtied

B. clean — broken

C. find — used

D. dirty — cleaned

E. wipe — scratched

15.

 is to as is to:

A   B   C   D   E

16.

Grass is to **plain** as:

A. Water is to ocean.

B. Sand is to beach.

C. Polar bear is to glacier.

D. Root is to tree.

E. Stem is to flower.

17.

The numbers in each box go together following the same rule. Figure out that rule and then apply it to the third box. What number goes where you see the question mark?

| 1, 2, 8 | | 2, 4, 16 | | 3, 6, ? |

A. 24   **B.** 18   **C.** 20   **D.** 12   **E.** 8

18.

A meal cannot be eaten without:

A. friends   **B.** food   **C.** a cafeteria   **D.** forks   **E.** a beverage

19.

If the words were arranged to make the **best** sentence, with which letter would the **second** word of the sentence begin?

| found | Sarah | never | toy's | batteries | the |

A. s   **B.** n   **C.** f   **D.** t   **E.** b

20.

The drawings in the box go together in a certain way. Which drawing goes where you see the question mark?

A   B   C   D   E

21.

The numbers in each box go together following the same rule. Figure out that rule and then apply it to the third box. What number goes where you see the question mark?

| 2, 8 | | 3, 12 | | ?, 20 |

A. 8   **B.** 6   **C.** 5   **D.** 4   **E.** 10

22.

What comes next in the series?   A   11   C   13   E   15   G   17   ?

A. J   **B.** 19   **C.** H   **D.** I   **E.** 18

23.

The numbers in each box go together following the same rule. Figure out that rule and then apply it to the third box. What number goes where you see the question mark?

| 9, 12, 15 | 7, 10, 13 | 5, ?, 11 |

A. 7   **B.** 8   **C.** 10   **D.** 12   **E.** 9

24.

The words in the box go together in a certain way. Which word goes where you see the question mark?

| cart | catastrophe | caramel |
| shirt | shame | ? |

A. same   **B.** carousel   **C.** shallow   **D.** savior   **E.** silhouette

25.

The opposite of **clean** is:

A. old   **B.** new   **C.** spotless   **D.** dirty   **E.** rusted

26.

Todd won more prizes at the arcade than Matthew, but fewer than Spencer. If Todd won eight prizes, two of which were toys and four of which were candy, we know for certain that:

A. Spencer spent the most money at the arcade.

B. Mathew likes toys more than candy.

C. Spencer won at least three toys.

D. Matthew didn't win any prizes.

E. Spencer won at least nine prizes total.

27.

Stacy has thirty-four papers in a pile. Some of the papers are red, some a green, and some are blue. Stacy has ten red papers. If she has three times as many green papers as blue papers, how many green papers does she have?

A. 12   **B.** 9   **C.** 30   **D.** 8   **E.** 18

28.

The numbers in the box go together in a certain way. Which number goes where you see the question mark?

3	14	18
4	21	?
5	28	36

A. 30   **B.** 3   **C.** 29   **D.** 24   **E.** 27

29.

If the words were arranged to make the **best** sentence, with which letter would the **third** word of the sentence begin?

class	we	in	met	science

A. w   **B.** m   **C.** i   **D.** s   **E.** c

30.

We were all surprised that she wore such a(n) _____ dress to the dance because she usually dressed plainly.

A. unique   **B.** severe   **C.** simple   **D.** fancy   **E.** feminine

31.

Which word does **not** go with the others?

A. oak   **B.** pine   **C.** acorn   **D.** maple   **E.** willow

32.

What number is missing in this series?   29   13   27   13   ?   13   23   13   21

A. 15   **B.** 11   **C.** 25   **D.** 24   **E.** 26

33.

The drawings in the box go together in a certain way. Which drawing goes where you see the question mark?

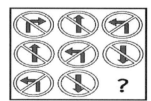

A   **B**   **C**   **D**   **E**

34.

The numbers in the box go together in a certain way. Which number goes where you see the question mark?

| 5,6 | 1,7 | 6,1,5,7 |
| 2,3 | ? | 3,4,2,9 |

A. 9,4   **B.** 2,9   **C.** 4,3   **D.** 4,9   **E.** 3,4

35.

 is to as is to:

                    A   **B**   **C**   **D**   **E**

36.

What number is five less than three times seven?

A. 8   **B.** 33   **C.** 16   **D.** 26   **E.** 11

37.

Coffee is to **beverage** as **pie** is to:

A. meal   **B.** dinner   **C.** snack   **D.** dessert   **E.** blueberry

38.

What goes where you see the question mark in this
series?   E   7   2   G   12   5   I   19   10   K   ?   16

A. M   **B.** 27   **C.** 23   **D.** 28   **E.** 25

39.

The numbers in the box go together in a certain way. Which number goes where you see the question mark?

| 5 | 18 | 31 |
| 11 | 24 | ? |

A. 32   **B.** 29   **C.** 35   **D.** 40   **E.** 37

40.

The words in the box go together in a certain way. Which word goes where you see the question mark?

eat	beat	seat
ate	?	sate

A. bate   **B.** bare   **C.** feat   **D.** fate   **E.** arts

41.

The drawings in the box go together in a certain way. Which drawing goes where you see the question mark?

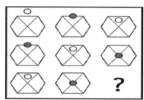

A   B   C   D   E

42.

Last school week, Mrs. Smith, Mr. Carter, and Ms. Davis all assigned homework. Mrs. Smith assigned homework each day except Thursday. If Mr. Carter assigned less homework than Mrs. Smith but more than Ms. Davis, then we know for certain that:

A. Ms. Davis didn't assign any homework.

B. Mr. Carter didn't assign homework on Thursday.

C. Mr. Carter assigned homework a maximum of three days.

D. Ms. Davis assigned homework two days.

E. Mr. Carter assigned homework two days.

43.

What number comes next in this series?   7   18   14   25   21   32   ?

A. 30   **B.** 18   **C.** 24   **D.** 22   **E.** 28

44.

 is to as is to:

A   B   C   D   E

45.

The opposite of **hot** is:

A. fire   B. cold   C. cool   D. snow   E. warm

46.

Madison has sixty books on her bookshelf. Some of the books are fiction books and the others are nonfiction. If she has four times as many fiction books as nonfiction books, how may fiction books does she have?

A. 20   B. 40   C. 48   D. 12   E. 24

47.

If the words were arranged to make the **best** sentence, with which letter would the **first** word of the sentence begin?

| at | house | party | Timothy's | the | will | be |

A. t   B. h   C. p   D. w   E. b

48.

The drawings in the box go together in a certain way. Which drawing goes where you see the question mark?

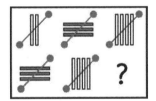

A   B   C   D   E

49.

A book cannot be read without:

A. a teacher   B. a story   C. people   D. words   E. pictures

50.

The drawings below form a series. Which drawing continues that series and goes where you see the question mark?

A   B   C   D   E

51.

The numbers in the box go together in a certain way. Which number goes where you see the question mark?

9	12	15
11	14	?

A. 17   B. 16   C. 18   D. 19   E. 13

52.

The drawings below form a series. Which drawing continues that series and goes where you see the question mark?

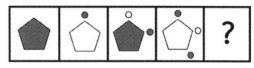

A   B   C   D   E

53.

After Lori fired some of her employees, she had to _____ work on the project until she could hire more people.

A. inspire   B. postpone   C. gift   D. start   E. alternate

54.

 is to as is to:

A   B   C   D   E

55.

Larry has several different apps on his phone.Each of the apps is one of three types: some of the apps are games, while others are educational, and some are for reading the news. If Larry has a total of twelve apps and three of them are games, we know for certain that:

A. Larry likes to read the news more than use games.

B. Larry doesn't use games very often.

C. He does not have the same number of educational and news apps

D. Larry spent a lot of money on apps for his phone.

E. Larry has a total of four news apps.

56.

The numbers in each box go together following the same rule. Figure out that rule and then apply it to the third box. What number goes where you see the question mark?

| 2, 14 | 3, 21 | 4, ? |

A. 24   **B.** 28   **C.** 26   **D.** 30   **E.** 32

57.

The words in the box go together in a certain way. Which word goes where you see the question mark?

| sag | slug | stung |
| bat | belt | ? |

A. swift   **B.** ban   **C.** bolt   **D.** blurt   **E.** start

58.

A piano cannot be played without:

A. a song   **B.** fingers   **C.** a conductor   **D.** singing   **E.** music sheets

59.

The numbers in the box go together in a certain way. Which numbers go where you see the question marks?

3	18	9
?	36	18
7	42	?

A. 6, 22   **B.** 5, 25   **C.** 4, 24   **D.** 4, 21   **E.** 6, 21

60.

 is to as is to:

A   B   C   D   E

61.

The drawings below form a series. Which drawing continues that series and goes where you see the question mark?

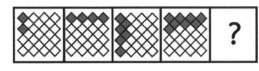

A   B   C   D   E

62.

Which word does **not** go with the others?

A. addition   **B.** subtraction   **C.** multiplication   **D.** division   **E.** fractions

63.

What number is four more than six times eight?

A. 52   **B.** 32   **C.** 44   **D.** 20   **E.** 54

64.

The drawings below form a series. Which drawing continues that series and goes where you see the question mark?

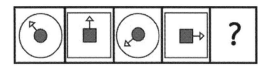

     A   **B**   **C**   **D**   **E**

65.

Which word does **not** go with the others?

A. jump   **B.** pounce   **C.** leap   **D.** spring   **E.** skip

66.

The drawings in the box go together in a certain way. Which drawing goes where you see the question mark?

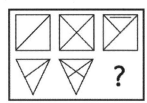

     A   **B**   **C**   **D**   **E**

67.

The numbers in each box go together following the same rulE. Figure out that rule and then apply it to the third box. What number goes where you see the question mark?

| 2, 6 | | 4, 9 | | 6, ? |

A. 8   **B.** 10   **C.** 9   **D.** 12   **E.** 13

68.

The opposite of **enter** is:

A. in   **B.** go   **C.** exit   **D.** entrance   **E.** finish

69.

The numbers in each box go together following the same rulE. Figure out that rule and then apply it to the third box. What number goes where you see the question mark?

| 12, 3 | | 20, 5 | | 32, ? |

A. 8   **B.** 6   **C.** 9   **D.** 4   **E.** 7

70.

The numbers in the box go together in a certain way. Which number goes where you see the question mark?

| 23 | 18 | 13 |
| 19 | 14 | ? |

A. 5   **B.** 10   **C.** 9   **D.** 8   **E.** 11

71.

 is to as is to:

A   B   C   D   E

72.

The numbers in the box go together in a certain way. Which number goes where you see the question mark?

| 32 | 8 | 2 |
| 48 | 12 | ? |

A. 8   **B.** 2   **C.** 4   **D.** 6   **E.** 3

Answer Key Practice Test 2

Number	Correct Answer	Type of Question	Number	Correct Answer	Type of Question
1	E	antonym	37	D	verbal analogy
2	A	pattern matrix	38	B	number series
3	A	verbal analogy	39	E	number matrix
4	C	figural series	40	A	word matrix
5	D	logical selection	41	B	pattern matrix
6	B	sentence completion	42	C	inference
7	A	verbal classification	43	E	number series
8	C	inference	44	C	figural analogy
9	C	figural analogy	45	B	antonym
10	B	sentence arrangement	46	C	arithmetic reasoning
11	A	verbal analogy	47	A	sentence arrangement
12	C	word matrix	48	E	pattern matrix
13	E	figural series	49	D	logical selection
14	A	sentence completion	50	E	figural series
15	C	figural analogy	51	A	number matrix
16	B	verbal analogy	52	B	figural series
17	A	number series	53	B	sentence completion
18	B	logical selection	54	D	figural analogy
19	E	sentence arrangement	55	C	Inference
20	E	pattern matrix	56	B	number series
21	C	number series	57	D	word matrix
22	D	number series	58	B	logical selection
23	B	number series	59	E	number matrix
24	C	word matrix	60	D	figural analogy
25	D	antonym	61	E	figural series
26	E	inference	62	E	verbal classification
27	E	arithmetic reasoning	63	A	arithmetic reasoning
28	E	number matrix	64	E	figural series
29	C	sentence arrangement	65	E	verbal classification
30	D	sentence completion	66	A	pattern matrix
31	C	verbal classification	67	D	number series
32	C	number series	68	C	antonym
33	C	pattern matrix	69	A	number series
34	D	number matrix	70	C	number matrix
35	D	figural analogy	71	B	figural analogy
36	C	arithmetic reasoning	72	E	number matrix

Answers Explanations Practice Test 2

1.   Correct Answer: E

This question is looking for the antonym of the word <u>novice</u>, which means a beginner. Students may be tempted to choose answer D, as someone who is the opposite of a beginner may be professional; however, this is not a true opposite. Choice E is the only answer that makes sense.

2.   Correct Answer: A

As we progress from left to right, the pattern in the top row shows that the small circle in the square moves from the top-left position to the bottom-right and then to the top-right. At the same time it alternates its highlighting from dark to light and then back to dark. The same pattern applies on the second row. The square inside the circle will move from the top-left position to the bottom-right and then to the top-right. It will also alternate its highlighting. Therefore, the missing figure in the second position must be a circle, eliminating choices C and D. The small square must be positioned inside in the bottom-right position, which eliminates choice B. Only choices A and E remain. The correct choice is A, because the square must alternate its highlighting from dark to light.

3.   Correct Answer: A

With this question, the key is to figure out the relationship between the words provided in the analogy. It helps to put the words in a sentence to evaluate their relationship. We might say, that "many pages make up a book." We know, then, that this analogy shows us a very small part of a much larger whole. We can also say that "many bricks make up a building," which means that choice A is the correct answer. Concrete, option B, is incorrect because bricks are not a composite, or part of, concrete. The answer options C and D describe bricks, but they do not complete the part to whole analogy. Additionally, the answer option E of "fire" doesn't exhibit a clear relationship to bricks.

4.   Correct Answer: C

The first three drawings are all different from each other. The first drawing is a square, a circle, and a shaded hexagon; the second drawing is a hexagon, a shaded square, and a circle; and the third drawing is a shaded circle, a hexagon, and a square. We can also see that the fifth figure is the same as the second figure. This indicates that the group of the first three shapes starts to repeat, which means the fourth shape must also be the same as the first shape. Choice C is the same drawing as the first drawing in the series and completes the pattern of three different figures that repeat.

5.   Correct Answer: D

With this question, the key is finding the answer option that is something all homes have. Students may want to choose options B or C, as these are likely things that homes often have. However, a home—like an apartment, for example—could be one room, so that would rule out answer option B. Additionally, while most homes do have a bed, it is possible that not all homes contain beds. The only answer that works is option D because, by definition, a home is a place where a person lives.

6.   Correct Answer: B

In answering this question, it's important to consider both of the blanks. The words used to fill these blanks have a cause and effect relationship, so students have to be alert for this correlation. The only set of answers that works is option B. However, there are several answer options where one word will make sense. For example, it would make sense to say that someone <u>passed</u> a test or <u>aced</u> a test; however, these answer options fall apart when we fill in the second blank. It would not make sense to say that someone <u>passed</u> a test because they did not <u>study</u>, or that someone <u>aced</u> a test because they did not <u>understand</u> the material. The other answer options—C and D—have answer options that don't really make sense in either blank.

7.   Correct Answer: A

With this question, we have to look for a pattern in the answer options. Most of the answers start with "sh" and ends with "s." We have: shackles, shirts, shades, and shakes. The only answer option that does not belong is <u>shine</u> because, though it starts with an "sh," it does not end with an "s." Therefore, this (choice A) is our correct answer, as this option is unlike the others.

8.   Correct Answer: C

Based on the information provided in this question, we know that the order of these girls' ages, from oldest to youngest, is Tiffany, Liza, then Madison. Other than this, we don't know anything for certain; everything else besides answer option C is a guess rather than a fact.

9.   Correct Answer: C

In the first pair of this figural analogy, we can see that the hexagon rotates by 180 degrees and then reverses its highlighting so that the light sections become dark and the dark sections become light. To find the missing figure, we must rotate the circle by 180 degrees and reverse its highlighting. By reversing the highlighting, the circle we are looking for will have only one of its sections unshaded. Answer A is eliminated, because it is a hexagon and not a circle. Answers B and D are also eliminated because they have more than one unshaded section. The correct answer is C because it has been rotated by exactly 180 degrees before reversing its highlighting.

10.   Correct Answer: B

In order to answer this question, students must first arrange the sentence correctly. The completed sentence should read, "Put your hand in mine." Then, students must identify the first letter of the second word of the sentence: "y." The correct choice is therefore option B.

11.   Correct Answer: A

We know that analogies are all about determining the relationship between words. If we make a sentence to show the relationship in this question, we might say that a "note is part of a scale." In looking at the answer options, students need to ask themselves what other pair of words would fit equally well in this sentence. Out of all the options, a "star is part of a constellation" makes the most sense. Therefore, choice A is the correct answer.

12.   Correct Answer: C

The key to this question is determining the relationship between the words. In the top row, each word, moving from left to right, has an additional letter. The base word is <u>on</u>. To get the next word, we've added a letter— an s— to the beginning, so we wind up with <u>son</u>. Then, we add another letter to the end of <u>son</u> to get <u>song.</u> When we move to the bottom row, we know that as we move from left to right, we will start with a base word. From the base word, we add a letter at the beginning to get the second word, and we add an additional letter to the end to get the third word. The word that would complete this scenario is <u>man</u>. Students might be tempted to choose answer B, <u>san;</u> however, we know that the answer option has to correspond with the third word in the row.

13.   Correct Answer: E

In this series, each drawing is made up of an inner and an outer shape. Each inner shape has an arrow attached, and the arrow rotates counterclockwise 90 degrees between each shape as we move from left to right. Therefore, we expect that the missing shape will be one with an arrow attached at the bottom of its inner shape. We can eliminate choices A and D because the arrow in these shapes is not at the bottom. In choice C the arrow is attached at the bottom of the outer shape rather than at the bottom of the inner shape. To make our final selection between choices B and E, we observe that the outer shapes of the given four drawings in this series are all different from each other: circle, square, hexagon and triangle. The hexagon outer shape in choice B has already been used as an outer shape in the third drawing of the series. Therefore, the missing drawing must be one with a new different outer shape, which is the diamond in choice E.

14.   Correct Answer: A

The key with this question is making sure that both words make sense in the given context. Any of the first words in the answer options would make sense: we can '<u>wash</u>', '<u>clean</u>', '<u>find</u>', '<u>dirty</u>' or '<u>wipe</u>' dishes. However, the second answer option must make sense together with the first word. Only the words in choice A work together in the blanks to make a complete thought.

15.   Correct Answer: C

In the first pair of this figural analogy, each of the two drawings is comprised of an outer shape and inner shape. The outer shape changes from a circle to a triangle and the inner shape stays the same, but changes from light to dark. Similar traits must be applied to the second pair, which has an outer shape that is a square and an inner shape that is a light circle. The outer shape must change from a square, which eliminates choice B. Choices A and D are eliminated because the circles inside do not change from light to dark. Choice E is eliminated because the inner shape is a square and not a circle. Only choice C has an outer shape that is different than a square and a circle that has changed from light to dark.

16.   Correct Answer: B

In figuring out this questions, students need to put the words of the analogy into a sentence. This helps with determining the relationship. We could say, "Grass is a small part of a plain." The only answer that also fulfills this relationship is option B, as we could say "sand is a small part of the beach." Students may be tempted to choose <u>water is to ocean</u>; however, this question goes beyond a simple part to whole relationship. The key is that the first item in the analogy is a very small, individual component of a much larger whole.

17. Correct Answer: A
The pattern in the first two boxes shows that the first number is multiplied by 2 to give the second number, and then the second number is multiplied by 4 to give the third number. In the first box 1x2=2 and 2x4=8. In the second box 2x2=4 and 4x4=16. Therefore, in the third box, 3x2=6 and 6x4=24, so the correct answer is A.

18. Correct Answer: B
The correct answer to this question is choice B because you cannot eat a meal unless you have food to eat. The other answer options might be a part of the meal-eating experience, but they are not vital to what makes a meal.

19. Correct Answer: B
Students can find this sentence by first grouping the words "Sarah found" and "the toy's batteries." Students can then figure out that the best place for the word "never" would be between "Sarah" and "found." The sentence, once arranged, should therefore be "Sarah never found the toy's batteries." Therefore, "never" is the second word, so the answer is option B as "n" is the first letter of the second word.

20. Correct Answer: E
In the top row, we can see that between the first two circles: a) the diagonal line changes direction (from upper-left to lower-right in the first circle, to lower-left to upper-right in the second circle) b) the small star changes position (from the top of the first circle to the bottom of the second circle) and c) the highlighting of the small star alternates (from light in the first circle to dark in the second circle). The third circle has all the traits of the previous two designs combined: two diagonal lines and two small stars. The highlighting again alternates from dark in the previous design to light. This pattern must be applied in the second row to find the second square. First of all, we eliminate choice C as it is a circle and not a square. We also eliminate choices A and B because the direction of the diagonal line does not change from the first design. Since the first square has a small dark arrow on the bottom, we need to find a square with a light arrow on top. Choices D and E both have a small arrow on top, but only in choice E does the arrow change to light. So, E is the correct answer.

21. Correct Answer: C
The pattern in the first two boxes shows that the second number is calculated by multiplying the first number by 4. In the first box 2x4=8. In the second box 3x4=12. You could also say that we can divide the second number by 4 to get the first number. In the first box 8/4=2. In the second box 12/4=3. Therefore, to get the missing number in the third box we can divide 20 by 4. Since 20/4=5, the correct answer is C.

22.   Correct Answer: D

This series is made up of alternating letters and two-digit numbers. The last number before the question mark is 17, which means that the missing term that follows must be a letter. Choices B and E can be eliminated since they are numbers. Focusing on just the letters, we can see that they progress by skipping every other letter starting from A as shown in the following pattern:

A B̸ C D̸ E F̸ G H̸ I ....

Since we will skip the letter that comes after G, the next letter must be I. The correct answer is D.

23.   Correct Answer: B

The pattern in the first two boxes shows that if we add 3 to the first number we get the second number, and if we add 3 to the second number we get the third number. In the first box 9+3=12 and 12+3=15. In the second box 7+3=10 and 10+3=13. Therefore, if we subtract 3 from the third number of the third box we will find the number that is missing: 11-3=8. To test the pattern in the third box we can use 5+3=8 and 8+3=11. The missing number is 8, which means the correct answer is B.

24.   Correct Answer: C

In order to answer this question, students must recognize that each of the words in the first row starts with "ca." If we apply this same rule to the second row, we know that each word must start with "sh." The only answer choice that works for this rule is option C.

25.   Correct Answer: D

This question asks students for the antonym of <u>clean</u>. Students might be drawn to the answer 'spotless'; however, this is a synonym rather than an antonym of <u>clean</u>. Additionally, though something <u>rusted</u> or <u>old</u> might not be <u>clean</u>, these answer choices aren't exactly the opposite of clean. The only true opposite in this question is answer choice D.

26.   Correct Answer: E

With this question, students must differentiate what *could* be true from what we know for certain is true. Based on the information provided, we know with certainty that Spencer has at least nine prizes because he has more prizes than Todd, who has eight total. The other answer options are assumptions that *could* be true but which aren't necessarily.

27.   Correct Answer: E

In order to answer this question, students need to tackle this problem step by step. First of all, we know that Stacy has a total of 34 papers. Of those, she has 10 red papers. Therefore, 24 of the papers must be either green or blue. We also know that she has 3 times as many green papers as blue papers. In order to figure out how many she has of each, students need to figure out that they are dealing with a 3:1 ratio. We're essentially dividing 24 into four parts (3 parts green, 1 part blue). We know that 24 divided by those 4 parts is 6. So, if Stacy has 3 parts green, we can multiply 3 x 6 to get 18. Therefore, option E is the correct answer.

28.   Correct Answer: E
There is no obvious algebraic relationship among the numbers of each row. Taking a look at the columns, we notice that in the second column the numbers are 14, 21, 28, which are all multiples of 7. Each of the numbers in the first column is one more than the number that was multiplied by 7 in the second column. For example, 2x7 = 14 and the number next to 14 on the left is 3 which is 1 more than 2. Similarly, 3x7=21 and the number on its left is 4 which is one more than 3. Therefore, we understand that if we subtract 1 from the first number and then multiply the difference by 7, we will get the second number. ((3-1) x7=14, (4-1)x7=21, (5-1)x7=28). Now that we have identified the rule between the first and second number in each row, we can determine whether a similar rule applies between the second and the third number, or maybe between the first and the third numbers. Looking at the third column we can see that if we subtract one from the first number and multiply the difference by 9, we will get the third number ((3-1)x9=18 and (5-1)x9=36). So, if we apply this rule in the second row we will find the missing number: (4-1)x9=3x9=27. Therefore, the correct answer is E.

29.   Correct Answer: C
In figuring out the answer to this question, students have to arrange the words into a sentence first. The key is figuring out which word would make the best subject of the sentence. We is the only word that would work well as a subject. Once students have figured out this first word, they then have to ask themselves which word could possibly follow this subject, and they may recognize that it should be a verb. Therefore, the only option in terms of a second word is met. From there, students should be able to complete the sentence. It should read, "We met in science class." Since the third word is in, we know that answer choice C is correct.

30.   Correct Answer: D
To figure out this sentence, students have to use context clues. The clue here is she usually dressed plainly. This should signal to us that, to fill in the blank, we need a word that is the opposite of plain. The best answer, then, is fancy. Students might be tempted to fill in the blank with unique or feminine; however, we once again have to go back to the key context clue. Neither of these words are really the opposite of plain.

31.   Correct Answer: C
In order to answer this question, we have to try and categorize the given answer choices. Each answer is a different type of tree, except for option C. Acorns come from trees but they aren't a type of tree themselves.

32.   Correct Answer: C
If we make pairs of numbers in this series, we will get four pairs (29 and 13, 27 and 13, ? and 13, and 23 and 13). The second number in each pair is always 13, and the first number in each pair is decreasing by 2 starting from 29. Since the missing number is the first number of the third pair, it must be 29-2-2=25. Therefore, the correct answer is C.

33. Correct Answer: C

In this pattern matrix, we see a series of circles with a diagonal line through them with shaded arrows inside. The arrows are curved when they point to the left or right and straight when pointing up or down. Also, in each row, the arrow changes its pointing direction counterclockwise by 90 degrees. For example, in the first row it starts pointing to the right, then upwards and then to the left. Since the drawing in the third row before the question mark has its arrow pointing down, we know we are looking for a drawing with an arrow pointing to the right. Therefore, we can eliminate choice D which has an arrow pointing to the left. We can also eliminate choice E because although the arrow is pointing to the right, it is not curved as it should be. Additionally, we can eliminate choice B because the arrow is drawn above the diagonal line of the circle instead of being behind it as in all drawings in the matrix. In order to choose among the remaining choices of A and C, students need to pay attention to the direction of the diagonal lines in the matrix. We see that when the arrow is pointing to the right, the diagonal has an upper-left to bottom-right direction. When the arrow is pointing to the left, the diagonal has an upper-right to bottom-left direction. Since we are also looking for a right pointing arrow, the direction of the diagonal must have an upper-left to bottom-right direction. Thus, the correct answer is C.

34. Correct Answer: D

In this number matrix, we need to identify the relationship between the two pairs of numbers and the series of four numbers. In the first row, we can see that the four number series is created by switching the numbers in the first pair to get the first and third number in the series of four numbers. The second and the fourth number in the series of four numbers are the second pair of numbers in their original order. The same pattern must be applied to the second row. The second and the fourth numbers in the four number series are 4 and 9, which is the pair of numbers we are looking for. Therefore, the correct answer is D.

35. Correct Answer: D

In the first pair of this figural analogy, we can see that the shape of the two combined triangles remains the same and the small circle inside stays in the same position but alternates from light to dark. A similar pattern must be applied to the second pair. The overall shape, which is a square with a vertical line, must remain the same. Choices B and E are eliminated as they are squares with horizontal lines. The triangle must be in the same position on the right but change from dark to light. Therefore, choice D is the correct answer.

36. Correct Answer: C

To answer this question, we must first figure out that 3x7=21. Then, we know that 21-5=16.

37. Correct Answer: D

As with all analogies, it is helpful to put the words into a sentence to discern their relationship. We could say, "coffee is a type of beverage." Our next step would be to say, "pie is a type of_____." Based on this, the only answer that works is dessert.

38.   Correct Answer: B

In this series of numbers and letters each letter is followed by a pair of numbers. The letter E is followed by the pair 7 2, the letter G is followed by the pair 12 5, etc. Since we are looking for what follows the letter K, we understand that this should be the first number of the pair of numbers. Choice A can be eliminated as it is a letter rather than a number. In order to find what number goes where the question mark is, we need to reveal the relationship between the numbers and the letters. Exploring the triple E 7 2, we observe that the difference between the numbers is 7-2=5, and E is the 5th letter of the alphabet. Moving to the triple G 12 5, we also see that the difference is 12-5=7 and G is the 7th letter of the alphabet. The pattern continues for the group I 19 10, where 19-10=9 and I is the 9th letter of the alphabet . Therefore, since K is the 11th letter of the alphabet, the number that follows it must be 11 greater than 16. Therefore, the missing number is 27 since 27-16=11 and K is the 11th letter of the alphabet. The correct answer is B.

39.   Correct Answer: E

The pattern in the first row of the box shows that we are adding 13 as we move from left to right (5+13=18 and 18+13=31). The same rule applies on the first two numbers in the second row (11+13=24). Therefore, since 13+24=37, the correct answer is E.

40.   Correct Answer: A

To figure out the answer to this question, students have to discover the pattern of the words in the box. Looking at the top row, we have the word eat in the first column. This serves as a base word in the pattern. The next word adds and a "b" to the beginning to get "beat." The third word adds an "s" to the base word to get "seat." We know then that, in the second row, we must follow the same pattern. So if ate is the base word, we need to add a "b" in the second column to get "bate." Since the third column also adds an "s" to the base word to get sate, we know the second row is adding the same letters to the base word as the first row. Option D may be a tempting answer, but it is not correct because the added letter must be a "b."

41.   Correct Answer: B

Each drawing in this pattern matrix is comprised of a hexagon with two diagonals and a small circle. In each row, as we progress from left to right, the small circle moves in a downward vertical direction. In the first row, it starts from outside of the hexagon, then moves down to the top of the hexagon, and then moves down again so that it is inside the upper triangle of the hexagon. In the second row, the small circle again moves downward from the top of the hexagon so that it is inside the upper triangle of the hexagon, and then moves down again so that it is at the center of the hexagon. At the same time, the circle alternates between light and dark as we go through the drawings in each row. The circle in the drawing in the third row before the question mark is located at the center of the hexagon. If it moves down, it will be inside the lower triangle of the hexagon. We also know that the next figure will have a light circle. We can eliminate choices C and D as they have dark circles. We can also eliminate choice E because the circle moved down too far, and choice A because the circle did not move. The only drawing with a light circle inside the hexagon at the bottom is B. Therefore, the correct answer is B.

42. Correct Answer: C

This question requires students to choose only the answer choice that provides information about something we know for certain. Based on the information provided in the question, we know that Mrs. Smith assigned homework on four days—Monday, Tuesday, Wednesday, and Friday. We also know that Mr. Carter assigned homework a maximum of three days, but we don't know which days for sure. We know that Ms. Davis may have assigned as many as two days of homework, but we don't know how many exactly or if she assigned homework at all. The only answer option was can say is true for certain is choice C.

43. Correct Answer: E

The pattern, moving from left to right, is to alternate addition of 11 and subtraction of 4 as shown below:

$$7 \ (+11) \ 18 \ (-4) \ 14 \ (+11) \ 25 \ (-4) \ 21 \ (+11) \ 32$$

Since 32-4=28, we can identify the correct answer as E.

44. Correct Answer: C

The first pair of this figural analogy has three circles inside the triangle for the first drawing and then three circles aligned horizontally in the second drawing. In the second drawing two of the circles have been move outside the triangle. Since the same pattern must be applied to the second pair of drawings, we need to find a drawing of a circle with three triangles aligned horizontally that has two of the triangles outside the circle and one triangle inside the circle. Choice D is eliminated because there are circles outside the circle rather than tri-angles. Choice E is eliminated because the triangle inside the circle has been rotated by 180 degrees. Choice A is eliminated because the triangles outside the circle are not the same as the one inside. Choice B is eliminated because the two triangles are partially inside the circle instead of being totally outside. Therefore, the correct answer is C.

45. Correct Answer: B

In figuring out the opposite of the word "hot", students have to keep in mind the difference between something that is hot versus merely warm. Hot is more of an extreme, so the an-swer is <u>cold</u> rather than <u>cool</u>. Though <u>snow</u> is cold, it isn't an exact opposite of hot. <u>Fire</u> and <u>warm</u> are related to the word <u>hot</u>, however, neither is the opposite of "hot".

46. Correct Answer: C

Students must figure out that this question is dealing with a total of five parts: 4 parts fiction books and 1 part nonfiction books. If we divide 60 books by 5 parts, we get 12. So, if Mad-ison has 4 times as many fiction books as nonfiction books, we know she has 12 nonfiction books and 48 fiction books.

47. Correct Answer: A

To answer this question, we first have to arrange the sentence. The best completed sen-tence in this question would read, "The party will be at Timothy's house." Based on this completed sentence, the first word is <u>the</u>. Therefore, since this starts with a "t," the correct answer is A.

48.   Correct Answer: E

Each figure in the first row of this pattern matrix is comprised of a specific number of thin bars that are crossed by a diagonal with a direction from bottom-left to upper-right. As we move from left to right the bars increase by one, alternate between light and dark, and alternate their direction between horizontal and vertical. Since the second drawing of the second row has four light vertical bars, students need to look for a shape with five dark horizontal bars. Choice A can be eliminated because it has four bars. Choice C and D can be eliminated because they have light bars. Choice B can also be eliminated because, although it has five highlighted and horizontal bars, the diagonal line that crosses the bars goes from up-left to bottom-right instead of up-right to bottom-left as is the case in all drawings. Therefore, the correct answer is E.

49.   Correct Answer: D

In order to read a book, you must read <u>words</u>. While a teacher, pictures, story, or other people might be part of the reading experience, they are not required to read a book.

50.   Correct Answer: E

In this series, each drawing is comprised of an outer shape that is filled with a group of identical smaller shapes. The outer shape alternates between a square and a hexagon. The number of the smaller inner shapes decreases by 1 as we move from left to right. The inner shapes also alternate between dark and light. The inner shape is never repeated between designs. Since the outer shape in the fourth drawing is a hexagon, we expect that the outer shape of the next drawing will be a square, so choice A is eliminated. As there are two stars inside the fourth drawing of the series we know that the missing drawing will have only one shape inside, so choice D can be eliminated. As the two stars inside the fourth drawing are light, we know that the drawing we are looking for will have one dark inner shape so choice C can be eliminated. Finally, choice B can also be eliminated, because the dark shape inside the square is a diamond, which was already used in the third drawing. Therefore, the correct answer is E

51.   Correct Answer: A

The pattern in the first row of the box shows that we are adding 3 as we move from left to right (9+3=12 and 12+3=15). The same rule applies on the first two numbers in the second row as 11+3=14. Therefore, since 14+3=17, the correct answer is A.

52.   Correct Answer: B

The main shape in this series is a pentagon that alternates between light and dark. Moving from left to right, one small circle is added to a vertex outside the pentagon starting at the top and moving in a clockwise direction. The small circles also alternate between light to dark as they are added, and their shading is reversed between drawings. The fifth drawing must have a dark pentagon, which eliminates choice C. An additional small circle at the lower-left vertex of the pentagon should be included in the fifth design, which eliminates choice E. The existing circles should be shaded the opposite of the fourth drawing, which eliminates choices A and D Therefore, the correct answer is B.

53. Correct Answer: B

Since Lori fired employees, we can assume she didn't have enough people to work on the project. We can assume, then, that she might <u>postpone</u>, or put off, working on the project until she hires more people.

54. Correct Answer: D

The first figure of the given pair in this figural analogy is a square which includes a triangle. The square has also a horizontal line which connects two opposite sides. Now, in the second figure of the given pair, the triangle becomes the outer shape with an inside square that has a horizontal line. The same pattern must be applied to the second pair too, which, in the first figure, has a triangle with a square and a vertical line. Students need to notice that the vertical line is a line of the triangle as it connects one of its vertices with the opposite side. Therefore, the figure that we are looking for must be a square which includes a triangle with a vertical line in it. Choices A and C can be eliminated as the outer shapes are triangles and not squares. Choice E can be eliminated because, although it is a square which includes a triangle, the vertical line is not a line of the triangle but of the square. Choice B can also be eliminated because, again, although we have a square which includes a triangle, the vertical line that is drawn is not a line of the triangle as it starts from the triangle's vertex but ends at the side of the square. Therefore, the correct choice is D.

55. Correct Answer: C

As with other inference questions, the key here is finding the answer that we know is true without any qualifications. We know that Larry has 12 apps; some are games, some educational, and some are for the news. Only 3 apps are games, so we know that there are 9 apps left. Of those 9 apps, some are educational and some are for the news. Since 9 cannot be divided evenly by the two types of apps, we know for certain there is not an even number of educational and news apps.

56. Correct Answer: B

The rule is that in each box, the first number is multiplied by 7 to get the second number (2x7=14 and 3x7=21). Multiplying the first number of the third box, by 7 we get 4x7=28. The correct answer is B.

57. Correct Answer: D

To answer this question, we have to find the pattern in the first row. Each of these words starts with the same letter—"s"— and ends with the same letter—"g." Additionally, each word has one more letter than the word before; the first word has three letters, the second has four letters, and the final word has five letters. We know that the second row must follow the same pattern. We know that it must start with a "b," end with a "t" and be five letters in length. The only word that fulfills all of these criteria is "blurt."

58. Correct Answer: B

The key here is the word <u>played.</u> A piano can only be played using <u>fingers</u>. Though a piano is often played with music sheets or in a musical composition suggestive of a song, someone could very well play the keys of a piano without forming a song.

59.   Correct Answer: E

In this pattern matrix, we have two missing numbers in two different rows. In the first row we can see that if we multiply the first number by 6 we get the second number (3x6=18), and if we divide the second number by 2 we get the third number (18/2=9). To determine if this is the pattern for the other rows, we move on by checking the rule partially. Dividing the last two numbers of the second row (36/2=18) shows that the second part of the rule is valid. Multiplying the first number of the third row by 6, we get the second number (7x6=42). Therefore, the pattern that we identified in the first row is also valid for the other two rows. In order to find the first number of the second row, we will divide the second number by 6 (36/6=6). In order to find the third number of the third row, we will divide the second number by 2 (42/2=21). Therefore, the correct answer is E.

60.   Correct Answer: D

In the first drawing on the left of this figural analogy, we have a hexagon as the outermost shape, a triangle as the middle shape, and a circle as the innermost shape. This drawing is paired with the drawing where the innermost circle has moved outside the shape, and the remaining two shapes (the hexagon and the triangle) have switched their positions. In addition, all three shapes reversed their shading. In the second pair the innermost square must move outside the shape and change from dark to light. Choice B is eliminated because the square is light and choice E is eliminated because a circle was moved outside the shape. Now, the diamond and the circle must switch places and reverse their shading. Choice A is eliminated because the circle and the diamond are both dark. Choice C is eliminated because the there is a pentagon inside the circle instead of a diamond. Therefore, choice D is the correct answer.

61.   Correct Answer: E

In this series, the number of shaded diamonds increases by 2 as we progress form left to right. The shaded diamonds also alternate their direction from vertical to horizontal. Additionally, when aligned vertically, the shaded diamonds are on the left side of the grid and when aligned horizontally they are on the top part of the grid. Since the fourth drawing has 8 shaded diamonds aligned horizontally, we expect that the missing drawing will have 10 shaded diamonds aligned vertically. Choice B is eliminated because the 10 shaded diamonds are aligned horizontally. Neither choice A or C has 10 shaded diamonds, so they are eliminated. Choices D and E both have 10 shaded diamonds aligned vertically, but in choice D, the shading is along the right side of the grid, so choice D is eliminated. Choice E is the correct answer.

62.   Correct Answer: E

While each of these words has to do with math, <u>fractions</u> are not a process in the same way that <u>addition</u>, <u>subtraction</u>, <u>multiplication</u>, and <u>division</u> are.

63.   Correct Answer: A

In order to answer this question, we must figure out that 6 x 8 = 48. Then, 48 + 4 = 52.

64. Correct Answer: E

In this series, each drawing is either an outer circle containing a smaller circle with an arrow attached, or an outer square containing a smaller square with an arrow attached. The drawings alternate between circles and squares. Since the fourth drawing is a square we expect that the missing drawing will be a circle, so choice C is eliminated. Choice B is also eliminated because it is a circle with a square inside instead of a circle. The arrows between the two circles drawings rotate counterclockwise 90 degrees, so the next position should be at the bottom-right side of the circle. Choice A and D are eliminated because the arrows did not rotate 90 degrees. The correct answer is E.

65. Correct Answer: E

This question requires students to figure out the nuances among these words. <u>Jump</u>, <u>pounce</u>, <u>leap</u>, and <u>spring</u> are all synonyms. However, the word <u>skip</u> is slightly different because it has to do with bouncing back and forth from one foot to another. So, while it is similar, it is not an exact synonym for the other words.

66. Correct Answer: A

In the first row of this matrix, as we move from left to right, students need to notice that initially there is a diagonal in the square from the lower-left to the upper-right. Then a diagonal from the upper-left to the lower-right is added. Finally, the bottom-right part of this diagonal is cut and placed next to the top side of the square. This pattern must be applied to the second row too, where we have a triangle which initially has a right to left diagonal segment inside and then it also gets a left to right diagonal segment which intersects with the first one. Therefore, the third drawing must be a triangle with the bottom right piece of the diagonal segment transferred next to the top side of the triangle. Choice D is eliminated because it is a square. Choice B is eliminated because no piece of either diagonal segment has been cut. Choice C is eliminated because both the bottom parts of the two diagonal segments have been removed. Choice E is eliminated because the bottom left piece of a diagonal segment has been cut and transferred instead of the bottom right segment of the other diagonal. Therefore, the correct answer is A.

67. Correct Answer: D

If we add 4 to the first number of the first box we will get the second number (2+4=6). In the second box, if we add 5 to the first number we will get the second number (4+5=9). Therefore, the pattern in the first two boxes shows that the number that is added to the first number of each box increases by 1 as we move from left to right. So, in order to find the second number in the third box, we need to add 6 to the first number. Since 6+6=12, the correct answer is D.

68. Correct Answer: C

If <u>enter</u> means to "go in," then we need a word that means to "go out." Therefore, <u>exit</u> is the best answer choice. Students might be distracted by <u>in</u>, <u>entrance</u>, or <u>go</u> but these are not the correct answers because they are closer to synonyms than antonyms. Additionally, <u>finish</u> is not correct as it has no real correlation to enter.

69. Correct Answer: A
The pattern in the first two boxes shows that the second number is obtained by dividing the first number by 4 (12/4=3 and 20/4=5). Therefore, if we divide 32 by 4 we will get the missing number. Since 32/4=8, the correct answer is A.

70. Correct Answer: C
The pattern in the first row of the box shows that we are subtracting 5 as we move from left to right (23-5=18 and 18-5=13). The same rule applies on the first two numbers in the second row (19-5=14). Since 14-5=9, the correct answer is C.

71. Correct Answer: B
In the first drawing on the left of this figural analogy, we have an unshaded hexagon with a shaded triangle inside. This drawing is paired with a drawing where the triangle has moved to the top outside of the hexagon and both shapes have reversed their shading. The same pattern must be applied to the second pair, which means that we are looking for a shaded triangle with an unshaded diamond above its vertex on top. Choices C and E are eliminated because the base figure is not a triangle. Choice A is eliminated because the triangle is not shaded. Choice D is eliminated because the shape above the triangle's vertex at the top is a pentagon and not a diamond. Therefore, the correct answer is B.

72. Correct Answer: E
The pattern in this matrix is that we divide each number by 4 to find the next one in the same row (32/4=8 and 8/4=2 for the first row and 48/4=12 for the second row). To find the missing number we divide 12 by 4, which equals 3. The correct answer is E.

Origins Publications

Use a No. 2 Pencil.
Fill-in Bubble Completely.
Ⓐ Ⓑ Ⓒ ⬤ Ⓔ

Name: _____   Date: _____

1. Ⓐ Ⓑ Ⓒ Ⓓ Ⓔ   19. Ⓐ Ⓑ Ⓒ Ⓓ Ⓔ   37. Ⓐ Ⓑ Ⓒ Ⓓ Ⓔ   55. Ⓐ Ⓑ Ⓒ Ⓓ Ⓔ
2. Ⓐ Ⓑ Ⓒ Ⓓ Ⓔ   20. Ⓐ Ⓑ Ⓒ Ⓓ Ⓔ   38. Ⓐ Ⓑ Ⓒ Ⓓ Ⓔ   56. Ⓐ Ⓑ Ⓒ Ⓓ Ⓔ
3. Ⓐ Ⓑ Ⓒ Ⓓ Ⓔ   21. Ⓐ Ⓑ Ⓒ Ⓓ Ⓔ   39. Ⓐ Ⓑ Ⓒ Ⓓ Ⓔ   57. Ⓐ Ⓑ Ⓒ Ⓓ Ⓔ
4. Ⓐ Ⓑ Ⓒ Ⓓ Ⓔ   22. Ⓐ Ⓑ Ⓒ Ⓓ Ⓔ   40. Ⓐ Ⓑ Ⓒ Ⓓ Ⓔ   58. Ⓐ Ⓑ Ⓒ Ⓓ Ⓔ
5. Ⓐ Ⓑ Ⓒ Ⓓ Ⓔ   23. Ⓐ Ⓑ Ⓒ Ⓓ Ⓔ   41. Ⓐ Ⓑ Ⓒ Ⓓ Ⓔ   59. Ⓐ Ⓑ Ⓒ Ⓓ Ⓔ
6. Ⓐ Ⓑ Ⓒ Ⓓ Ⓔ   24. Ⓐ Ⓑ Ⓒ Ⓓ Ⓔ   42. Ⓐ Ⓑ Ⓒ Ⓓ Ⓔ   60. Ⓐ Ⓑ Ⓒ Ⓓ Ⓔ
7. Ⓐ Ⓑ Ⓒ Ⓓ Ⓔ   25. Ⓐ Ⓑ Ⓒ Ⓓ Ⓔ   43. Ⓐ Ⓑ Ⓒ Ⓓ Ⓔ   61. Ⓐ Ⓑ Ⓒ Ⓓ Ⓔ
8. Ⓐ Ⓑ Ⓒ Ⓓ Ⓔ   26. Ⓐ Ⓑ Ⓒ Ⓓ Ⓔ   44. Ⓐ Ⓑ Ⓒ Ⓓ Ⓔ   62. Ⓐ Ⓑ Ⓒ Ⓓ Ⓔ
9. Ⓐ Ⓑ Ⓒ Ⓓ Ⓔ   27. Ⓐ Ⓑ Ⓒ Ⓓ Ⓔ   45. Ⓐ Ⓑ Ⓒ Ⓓ Ⓔ   63. Ⓐ Ⓑ Ⓒ Ⓓ Ⓔ
10. Ⓐ Ⓑ Ⓒ Ⓓ Ⓔ   28. Ⓐ Ⓑ Ⓒ Ⓓ Ⓔ   46. Ⓐ Ⓑ Ⓒ Ⓓ Ⓔ   64. Ⓐ Ⓑ Ⓒ Ⓓ Ⓔ
11. Ⓐ Ⓑ Ⓒ Ⓓ Ⓔ   29. Ⓐ Ⓑ Ⓒ Ⓓ Ⓔ   47. Ⓐ Ⓑ Ⓒ Ⓓ Ⓔ   65. Ⓐ Ⓑ Ⓒ Ⓓ Ⓔ
12. Ⓐ Ⓑ Ⓒ Ⓓ Ⓔ   30. Ⓐ Ⓑ Ⓒ Ⓓ Ⓔ   48. Ⓐ Ⓑ Ⓒ Ⓓ Ⓔ   66. Ⓐ Ⓑ Ⓒ Ⓓ Ⓔ
13. Ⓐ Ⓑ Ⓒ Ⓓ Ⓔ   31. Ⓐ Ⓑ Ⓒ Ⓓ Ⓔ   49. Ⓐ Ⓑ Ⓒ Ⓓ Ⓔ   67. Ⓐ Ⓑ Ⓒ Ⓓ Ⓔ
14. Ⓐ Ⓑ Ⓒ Ⓓ Ⓔ   32. Ⓐ Ⓑ Ⓒ Ⓓ Ⓔ   50. Ⓐ Ⓑ Ⓒ Ⓓ Ⓔ   68. Ⓐ Ⓑ Ⓒ Ⓓ Ⓔ
15. Ⓐ Ⓑ Ⓒ Ⓓ Ⓔ   33. Ⓐ Ⓑ Ⓒ Ⓓ Ⓔ   51. Ⓐ Ⓑ Ⓒ Ⓓ Ⓔ   69. Ⓐ Ⓑ Ⓒ Ⓓ Ⓔ
16. Ⓐ Ⓑ Ⓒ Ⓓ Ⓔ   34. Ⓐ Ⓑ Ⓒ Ⓓ Ⓔ   52. Ⓐ Ⓑ Ⓒ Ⓓ Ⓔ   70. Ⓐ Ⓑ Ⓒ Ⓓ Ⓔ
17. Ⓐ Ⓑ Ⓒ Ⓓ Ⓔ   35. Ⓐ Ⓑ Ⓒ Ⓓ Ⓔ   53. Ⓐ Ⓑ Ⓒ Ⓓ Ⓔ   71. Ⓐ Ⓑ Ⓒ Ⓓ Ⓔ
18. Ⓐ Ⓑ Ⓒ Ⓓ Ⓔ   36. Ⓐ Ⓑ Ⓒ Ⓓ Ⓔ   54. Ⓐ Ⓑ Ⓒ Ⓓ Ⓔ   72. Ⓐ Ⓑ Ⓒ Ⓓ Ⓔ

Made in the USA
Las Vegas, NV
08 December 2020

12324581R00042